Conversations with PHANTOMS

Exclusive Interviews About the 1978 TV Movie
KISS MEETS THE PHANTOM OF THE PARK

by Ron Albanese

Conversations with Phantoms:
Exclusive Interviews About the 1978 TV Movie
KISS MEETS THE PHANTOM OF THE PARK

By Ron Albanese

Copyright © 2020 Ron Albanese

No part of this book may be reproduced in any form or by any means, electronic, mechanical, digital, photocopying, or recording, except for inclusion of a review, without permission in writing from the publisher or Author.

Published in the USA by:
BearManor Media
4700 Millenia Blvd.
Suite 175 PMB 90497
Orlando, FL 32839
www.bearmanormedia.com

Paperback ISBN: 978-1-62933-600-8
Case ISBN: 978-1-62933-601-5

BearManor Media, Orlando, Florida
Printed in the United States of America
Book design by Ron Albanese
Edited by Ron Albanese

CONTENTS

Interviews

Kiss Management and Back Office:
Bill Aucoin 1
CK Lendt 15

Creating The Look, and Capturing It:
James Hulsey 25
Barry Levine 36

It All Starts With a Script:
Jan-Michael Sherman 43
Don Buday 51

Movie Makers:
Terry Morse 58
Deke Heyward 69
Gordon Hessler 82

On Screen:
Carmine Caridi 100
Don Lewis 107
Mary Kay Morse 115
Michael Bell 121
Lisa Jane Persky 130

About the Author 145

"Lay off, man. We make our fun the
way we want. Get it?" — Chopper

MORE CONTENTS

Phantom Findings

The Four Who Must Be One 14
Ducking Away from My Work 24
Gene Wasn't The Only One To Break A Wall 66
How Kiss Went Camping, Thanks To Abner's Uncle 80
Which Kiss Member Has The Greatest Powers? 95
A Lost, Powerful Character 106
Oddities and More 117
Peter's Pronunciation verses "Peter's Pronunciation" 128
Most of This Movie is Garbage ... Cans 140

"In a short time, the only laughing in my park will be that of the gods" — Abner

"Pretty mystical!" — Melissa

"Ack!"— Space Ace

Bill Aucoin
Kiss Manager, 1973-82
Interview conducted March 24, 2001

Formally interviewing Mr. Aucoin happened in person at a hotel in Rhode Island, where he was appearing at a Kiss convention. Our *Kiss Meets* ... convo was rife with topical drifts, due in equal parts to Bill's loquacious nature, and his indulging of your author's abundant enthusiasm. After a while, we decided to get something to eat, and set out into suburbia, which became its own little mini-tale.

1980's and early-to-mid '90's Kiss lead guitarist Bruce Kulick was also appearing at the Kiss exhibition, and he decided to tag along with us *(I recall his navigating around my son's car seat climbing into the car!)*. After I failed to get us a table in a packed, upscale restaurant *(oh, how strong the urge the was to shout out, "but Bill Aucoin is with me!")*, we settled on a small Italian place. It was soon pizza, red wine in paper cups, and rock 'n' roll, at the local pie joint. Bruce showed us the artwork to his then-upcoming *Audiodog* album, and it was total Kiss coolness watching Bill thoughtfully checking it out.

Bill's early 2000s recollections and personal feelings about *Kiss Meets* ... and the band overall run consistent to what he has always said, before and after; Kiss is more than a rock group, and doing a movie was a perfect next step — even if not a perfect movie. Also evident was his diplomatic nature regarding the band members — he truly loved *all* of the guys, equally.

For some long-lost reason *(primitive technology?)*, the interview tape begins with our talk already in progress, on the surprising topic of Kiss' *Dressed to Kill* album cover, which famously features the band in suits, and some funny footwear.

Ron *(about Gene's getup)*: I always liked the clogs — they sort of stick out.

Bill Aucoin: I can't remember the clogs, but I remember the suit. They might have been my clogs from Europe.

Ron: Peter actually had his own suit, right?

Bill: Oh, yeah. Peter always thought of himself as dapper *(thinking)* ... yeah, Peter always had good taste in clothing.

Ron: What kind of music did you listen to growing up? You don't strike me as a rock guy.

Bill: Not in total, no. But folk music, and rock. Pop rock, I guess.

Ron: Oh, like Bobby Sherman?

Bill *(laughing)*: No. My biggest music influence in college and high school was folk music.

Ron: So you were a hippie in college?

Bill: Yeah, a little. I ran a little coffee house in Boston, the Unicorn Coffeehouse on Boston Street. You know, the Chambers Brothers were the first crossover, taking folk into using electric guitars. And then Dylan came and saw them, and he played an electric guitar and was scolded for it ... uh, go ahead and ask me some Kiss movie questions!

Ron: I have asked you a lot already.

Bill: Go ahead and ask me again — let's see what we get!

Ron: The nucleus of the movie's story seems to have elements of the first Kiss comic book's tale, which came out in 1977.

Bill: Well, let me tell you the truth about the movie. The truth is that Hanna-Barbera got a deal to do a certain amount of movies of the week for NBC. Our agent at ATI, Jeff Franklin, had heard about it. He called me and said, "What do you think?" I said yeah, we could probably do it. It made sense, we were thinking that way anyway, to do something in film, whether it was an animated thing or not, we weren't sure. This would give us an opportunity to see exactly where the guys are in the sense of acting, whether or not it could be pulled off.

> "Let me tell you the truth about the movie."

We met with Hanna-Barbera's people, and they really had no clue about Kiss! They knew they were selling records, they knew they were getting publicity, but had *no clue*. So, I talked to them about what Kiss was about, obviously the comic book, and this and that. We actually sent Sean Delaney out to spend a few days with them, to give them an idea of what the characters were about. Sean not only helped to put their show together, he was their road manager initially; he really knew the characters. He also knew pretty much knew what they could, and could not, do. Maybe not quite as much as he thought (*laughs*). But in any case, we sent Sean out to say, "here's the characters, here's what Gene really means" because they didn't understand the characters. They really didn't. So [it was], "here's what Gene is, what Paul really is."

From that they gave us a script, which we revised a bit, but at that point they [Hanna-Barbera] had to commit to get something done for NBC. We were a little in that "Are we going to refine the script? Are we not going to refine the script?" area. It was like, "I guess it's good, it kind of works. If we want to do this, we have to do it [as is]." So we committed to do it.

"He didn't want to direct something that would be corny."

Ron: What were your initial impressions of the script?

Bill: I thought it was a little corny, but depending on how it was shot it could have been okay. Gordon Hessler was a real director. And later, he was taking his time to make sure every scene was really done well. He was also helping the guys learn what it means to be acting in front of a camera.

Ron: What exactly was his approach in coaching Kiss? Easy going? Disciplinarian?

Bill: He was hard on them, but he knew that they had never done it, so he was really trying to make it the best it could be. He didn't want to direct something that would be corny. What happened was, the first week we fell way behind schedule, because he was taking his time. He knew that they [Kiss] needed the time to make it really work. Well, after that, Hanna-Barbera made a critical decision, that I also think was pretty critical for the guys, and that was: "Hey, we can't have Gordon Hessler, we'll never get through this movie." And they fired him, and they brought in a director who was known for getting things done. The whole thing with the networks — I'm not sure if you're aware of this — is you pretty much get three takes. If in three takes you don't get it, well too bad. One of those takes is going to work. Because you don't have time, you don't have months, or the budget.

Gordon wasn't taking that. He was really trying to teach them. He was being a professor as well as the director; teaching them about film, trying to get the best performance he could. Teaching them how to react to the camera *and* working on the script at the same time. Hanna-Barbera didn't buy that. They fired him; they brought in a guy who was basically a network director. One, two, three takes at the most, done — "next!" — no matter what. That's how we finished the film. I think in one respect it was good, because Peter and Ace were really getting frustrated. They did not want to hang around to do this. You get to makeup at eight in the morning, and you'd wait for four hours. You'd do five minutes of filming, set up, and you wait two more hours. That's the film industry, and that's how movies are made, and that's the way it is. That just drove Ace and Peter crazy. Peter especially, but Ace, too.

"It was just like, 'get it done.'"

(This seems to be an accurate story of what happened during the earliest part of shooting in terms of time being lost, and the resulting pressure. In addition, a cast member was replaced, as well as a cameraman. However, Gordon Hessler himself was not fired, and some have asserted that Gordon was actually brought in to save the day. Bill may have been simply mixing up names, but again, his general account seems to be spot-on)

Ron: In your opinion, did the project itself break up Kiss?

Bill: It was the movie, but [it was] on top of everything. It was already happening with Peter, between Peter, and Gene and Paul. The day that we finished the movie — and again, it was rush, rush, hurry, hurry — you could tell by the special effects Hanna-Barbera put in, even for the time [it was not good]. They put in cheap effects. It was just like, "get it done."

Ron: Were you watching the dailies while filming?

Bill: I was watching some of the dailies, and toward the end, it was *rush, rush, rush*. So we kind of got caught in a little bit of a trap there. But the idea was to take it and make it into a Saturday morning cartoon series, an animated series, that could grow. That was basically my plan, behind the scenes.

Ron: From your and the band's side, the movie didn't have that classic Kiss push behind it.

Bill: It was done, it came out, and *boom*. Everything happened so quickly, that we didn't have time to really do it. We really didn't have the rights to do it, either. Hanna-Barbera had the rights. It was a whole different thing. As we got involved, they still didn't know how big Kiss was or wasn't. They were kind of caught; they just didn't know. They were used to doing things their way, their characters. It just never really sunk into them. It just never did.

Ron: How about NBC? How did they feel about the project?

Bill: For the network, it was just another movie. It did well, and it wasn't thought of as a good movie, obviously. They thought it was kind of corny. And it was, in its own right. So, it was kind of dismissed. But the truth of the matter is, at that point we could have done a lot more, from that. And I had plans to do a lot more, but we were already in trouble within the group, with Peter and Ace, and Paul and Gene. Peter had gotten himself almost killed the last night of shooting. That was a tough one. From Gene and Paul's standpoint it was "Oh, Peter's an idiot."

> **"But the truth of the matter is, at that point we could have done a lot more."**

Ron: They were unforgiving?

Bill: Yeah, they were unforgiving. So it just made it worse. They didn't want to give Peter a chance to get himself together. All they talked about was getting rid of him. From that point of view, the movie didn't help the internal scene.

Ron: I've always heard that the group wasn't really talking to each other during filming.

Bill: Well, they were. But as Peter and Ace starting complaining about the long days and having to be in makeup for hours and hours, the separation came. Whereas, Gene was talking to every crew member — he wanted to be a movie star, so he was in love with it. Paul was kind in between; he understood the benefit of it and everything. Gene was making the most of it, because he was thinking in his head that he wanted to be in the movies. That's how it went. And Ace and Peter just wanted to get out of there.

Ron: How did some of the other actors on the set view Kiss?

Bill: They were very lucky; they all worked with the group. The two guys [Anthony Zerbe and Carmine Caridi] were especially very professional. They were tops, they were pros. They were very nice to the guys, they knew they were just beginning. They did the job very well, and they were pleasant.

Ron: How much time did you spend on the set?

Bill: I was there all the time. It was the fact that it became something of a horror story, with the traumas between them, which meant I really had to be there.

Ron: Do you recall any specific incidents?

Bill: Other than just complaining? It was so traumatic, getting called at three in the morning and being told Peter was in the hospital, with Fritz Postlethwaite *(Kiss' tour manager at the time)*. Then, going to the hospital. No one had told me how bad it was, or wasn't. Then, when I got there, I find out that Fritz was really the one that was seriously hurt, and Peter was kind of making the most of it. And, I'll never forget this: Peter was more concerned about his stash in the car! Anyway, he was okay, and Fritz had gotten burned from the car melting down. That car was a Porsche 928, and it was all fiberglass, and the whole car had melted.

> "It was so traumatic, getting called at three in the morning and being told Peter was in the hospital."

Ron: Besides that, no one walked out of doing a scene or anything?

Bill: No, besides the hemming and hawing, it's interesting that Peter and Ace were certainly professional enough to know they had to do it.

Ron: Any memories of the various *Kiss Meets ...* parties or related premieres?

Bill: I wouldn't call them that. It was a TV show, you know? The parties that we had when we in New York ... I used to throw major parties, when we were doing Madison Square Garden — the events were the key to my throwing big parties. I had a philosophy that we had to have parties that were not only fun, but also exciting, and could *last*. At parties, you sometimes stay for an hour and leave, and there are parties that are really a lot of fun. I used to throw them at health clubs. I'd get a great, unique health club, and bring in the best caterer — the food would be impeccable, just the best. I knew that some of the guests — the families, relatives — would stay to have the great food, meet everyone, and enjoy some music. By midnight they would be gone, and the real rock 'n' roll party would begin, and go until five in the morning. You had steam rooms, pools, hot tubs. It was a *real* rock 'n' roll party!

Ron: Wow. About the quasi-premieres, was the movie shown on a big screen?

Bill: No.

Ron: Chris Lendt's book describes some sort of viewing, where various band members were sinking into their chairs while watching it. Peter couldn't believe he had Plastic Man's voice.

Bill: Yeah. It's funny, Peter obviously didn't like it, but he always had something else that would be bothering him, emotionally.

Ron: In your opinion, why exactly did the overdubbing happen?

Bill: They kept saying that it was his voice quality — that it didn't cut through. That was definitely part of it, but I think it was more of the way he reacted to the script, and how he pronounced things.

Ron: Maybe he was delivering it with a lack of energy?

Bill: Well, it's possible. He just wanted to leave, he just didn't want to do it. Yeah, the energy certainly wasn't in the delivery.

Ron: The scriptwriters were telling me a story of going to New York City and delivering the script. They say the band had the chance to ask questions about it.

Bill: Right.

Ron: The said the only questions anyone had were pertaining to the number of lines given to each guy: "Gene has 78 lines, and I don't!"

Bill: They didn't really say that. They didn't really know how many lines there were, but it was obvious that Gene had more. Then, the truth of the matter is that wasn't correct, because Gene didn't really speak! But he *was* on camera more.

> **"You must realize Kiss is a unit. Don't separate them."**

Ron: Besides his one, none of them had their own solo scenes.

Bill: I think that was meant to be that way. In fact, I think we had a meeting with Hanna-Barbera, saying, "You must realize Kiss is a unit. Don't separate them. Kiss does things together, Kiss is an entity." And, I think that was correct. That was one of the things we told them: don't try to break up this unit — even though it was about to be broken up!

Ron: I heard that before Magic Mountain, another amusement park was considered.

Bill: Yeah — I forget what place it was. *(The location is contained in one of the scriptwriter's interviews — can you locate the location?)*

Ron: Magic Mountain was perfect.

Bill: Yes, they were used to film work.

Ron: Some of the film *Rollercoaster* was done there.

Bill: Hey, I just saw that about a month ago.

Ron: Do you feel there are certain similarities between it and the Kiss movie? It was only a year or so earlier.

Conversations with Phantoms

Bill: I'm sure that the writers had some familiarity.

(In addition to sharing a locale, though it was not totally lensed there, Rollercoaster has a "madman in an amusement park" theme albeit a bit grittier. It also features a band playing "the park," our park — the unlikely Sparks. There are also a couple of other similarities that probably did not influence the Kiss movie, such as the featuring of the Revolution ride and Michael Bell being an on-screen cast member. It just another one of those coincidental '70s madman/amusement park combo things, just like that 1979 two-part episode of Wonder Woman called "The Phantom of The Roller Coaster" also was ... hey, wait a minute!)

Ron: Do you recall how much Kiss made from the movie?

Bill: I can't remember. I haven't got a clue. Someone must have my Hanna-Barbera contract, because it was in my files in the warehouse that got sold off. Richie Ranno — ask him if he know where it is *(Ranno, of the formerly Bill-managed band Starz, was involved in buying the contents of a Kiss warehouse in the 1980s).*

Ron: Speaking to the aftermath of the movie, was any blame for the project not being exactly what the band members wanted or expected directed at you?

Bill: No, they never really did blame me.

Ron: I mean, what could they have expected, anyway?

Bill: I told them it was their first film, and if they wanted to do more, fine. Ace and Peter said no, Gene wanted to do everything, again, because he thought of himself as becoming a movie star, and Paul was kind of in between. I certainly would have liked to have gone further, which means we would have had to educate them, and they would have had to really learn how to act. It never would have happened with Ace and Peter; that just wasn't them. They were rock and rollers, used to doing things spontaneously. Paul was a little scared. I would later take him out to do another movie, which was a Garry Marshall movie, a spoof.

> **"No, they never really did blame me."**

Ron: Would this be *Young Doctors in Love*?

Bill Aucoin

Bill: Yeah, and the scene didn't make the movie. Paul tried, and it was a really simple scene. It was okay.

Ron: Was he wearing his *Elder* outfit for that?

Bill: Probably. I can't remember. The scene just wasn't funny, that's all.

Ron: Did you ever attend a showing of *Kiss Meets ...* overseas, upon its theatrical release?

Bill: No. It actually did a little bit of business in Australia. Everyone actually made out pretty well with that movie. If it is released on DVD, I suspect it will do well again.

Ron: Did Gene and Paul really try to write with Giorgio Moroder? *(Kiss' nod-to-disco "I Was Made For Loving You" song and video was edited into the international version of the film, and must have been on my mind.)*

Bill: No, but Giorgio tried to come up with an idea for them. Disco was so big at the time, and Neil (Bogart) said, "You gotta do it, it'll sell millions of records." So, Neil and I went to him, and asked if he could think of something, which never really happened. Then, I went to Desmond Child.

Ron: Of course, there was the dance-y "Strutter '78." That wasn't really re-recorded in total, right?

Bill: No, we remixed. Sean Delaney and Mike Stone spent days and days, to get that done in time for release.

Ron: And Sean was doing his *Highway* solo album at the time.

Bill: And, that's a hell of an album. It happened at a time when Casablanca was kind of in a transitional state. There are a lot of stories behind that one.

Ron: Was there every talk of a soundtrack record, or new songs of any kind, for *Kiss Meets The Phantom of The Park?*

Bill: No, there wasn't time.

Ron: I'm surprised you didn't do a cameo.

Bill: I know — I should have. I think I was just busy dealing with the crisis behind the scenes! And, look: it's not just that Peter and Ace were totally obstinate. There are people who cannot sit for hours, waiting and waiting. You really have to love it. You have to have something to do in between. It was easy for Gene, because he just wanted to be around it. He picks up things quickly, and the movie was his ballgame. And, the more it was Gene's thing, the less they wanted to do it, too, because the rift was happening.

Ron: Was timing a problem, in terms of band burnout? If they had done this movie two years earlier, would it have been better?

Bill: Nah, it might have been easier for them two years earlier, because everything was new, but in truth, they were real rock 'n' rollers. They liked to be spontaneous, and I love them for that, whereas Gene was more calculated.

Ron: After *Kiss Meets ...* were any actual offers coming into the office for Kiss to do more movies?

Bill: No. Let's face it: the acting wasn't good. Even with Gene, although he got away with it more, because of the character, and the electronic voice.

Ron: Being that Peter ended up being overdubbed, to me he somehow emerged as the best Kiss actor!

Bill: The expression was there.

Ron: There was actually a lot of talent connected to this movie. Anthony Zerbe —

Bill: — is a fine, fine, actor.

Ron: Carmine Caridi —

Bill: — is more of a television actor, but very professional, with a good sense of humor. He had a lot of jokes. He had some great stories.

Ron: How about the girl *(Deborah Ryan, as "Melissa")*?

Bill: It probably killed her career forever!

Ron: Were/are you aware of all the various language overdubs?

Bill: There were more than we thought, actually. I remember finding out, and we were like, "oh my God ...."

Ron: How many can you recall?

Bill: French, Italian, Japanese ... .

Ron: It was also dubbed in Australian! While the movie was being worked on, plans for the solo albums were being put into action.

Bill: That was really our main focus. We had convinced Neil that the albums should come out all together. Initially, the solo albums were supposed to come out one at a time.

Ron: In a staggered fashion?

Bill: It really made a lot of sense; there could be focus on one, then another. It would have probably been done every few months. I convinced Neil to put them out at once. Up until the time we released them, the energy and excitement were really there. Then, all of a sudden, mistakes were made. The advertising agency — Howard Marks — put out the wrong advertising. They mixed up the release of the ads. The first one they put out was announcing that the albums have gone gold, and they weren't out yet. Ironically, that was the beginning of the end. You know when something goes wrong, and then things start toppling over? Then, Handleman — which is a big record distributor — ordered just a million units. Neil just went crazy. He pressed up another million, and then another million and half. We just had more units out there, piled and piled up. It was a disaster. But you know what? Right from the beginning, it was like it wasn't meant to be. I mean, eventually, they all sold platinum, but right when that wrong advertisement first went out, it was like, "oh, boy." It just went downhill from there.

Ron: Well, at least Ace had the fluke hit *("New York Groove")*.

Bill: Actually, in truth, if Eddie Kramer was a real producer — he's a great engineer, but he's not a great producer — he could have made that single into a *real* hit. It was a hit —a quasi-hit, because it could have been bigger.

Ron: I was surprised to learn that in America, Peter's album had not one, but two, singles released from it. Perhaps this was because it was lagging, sales wise?

Bill: No, it wasn't that. Don't forget, Peter's album, in many respects, was the type of music that Neil Bogart grew up with. That was kind of that old rock 'n' roll music. There were a couple of songs on the album that we thought had a real good shot, but didn't happen. Neil said about it, "you know, this kind of works." It was the kind of music he understood.

Ron: Vini Poncia produced it, the album gets overwhelmingly panned, and nonetheless, Kiss records *Dynasty (1979)* with him.

Bill: Interestingly enough! Vini's a really good music person; a good producer, and he could emotionally deal with them. We didn't want to go back to Bob Ezrin.

Ron: Was he considered at that point?

Bill: I always considered Bob, because he's a genius. He was tough on them, and he knew what to do — whether they *(the band)* were there or not! Vini's easy going, but he still got a little crazy!

Postscript:

As you may be able to discern from his interview, in 2001 Bill still had much of the brio that he undoubtedly had when he talked a nascent Kiss into becoming their manager. He was also super-supportive of my *Kiss Meets ...* book endeavor, which was a jolt of confidence. Sometime later, we saw each other at an event, and while we were catching up, he said, "Ron, there's just no stopping you." Not only was he complementary and inspiring, Bill Aucoin was just cool.

Bill passed away in 2010. He clearly made his mark as one of the greatest rock and roll band managers of all time, and as such, should be inducted into the Rock 'n' Roll Hall of Fame *(the original Kiss members have been)*. If you agree, please sign the online petition urging them to do so, at petitions.com.

PHANTOM FINDINGS
The Four Who Must Be One

As per the adamant wishes of management, quite possibly band members (that would be Gene, at least), and probably by way of influences like the Fantastic Four and The Beatles, in *Kiss Meets ...* the Kiss members are always together.

This of course excuses the sequences where Abner is shown building Evil Gene, and later, when he/it goes on a wall bustin', security guy tossin', and Coca-Cola stand smashin' rampage — that is not *our* Demon.

While it could have been cool to see the guys get to act as Kiss superheroes, solo — or if at the least, we were treated to seeing the Demon's feeding time, which one could imagine Space Ace not being around for — it was good sense to cluster Kiss. It kept things simple. If Paul had gone off alone with Melissa or something, the writers would have had to figure out how to get him back with the others for a group scene, which also may have wasted time. Additionally, not a single one of the Kiss guys could have carried a scene by themselves.

So, always we get all four, of a certain kind. But are they equal? A later *Phantom Findings* will reveal that in terms of superhero powers, there are interesting differences and disparities between them — and Paul just may the most powerful Kiss member!

C.K. Lendt
Kiss Business Associate, 1976-1988
Interview conducted April 12, 2001

Fresh out of college, Chris *(that's his a.k.a.)* joined the business end of the Kiss organization (Glickman-Marks*) in 1976. He was there for a bulk of the group's initial 1970's heyday, subsequent popularity dip, departures of original band members, desperate fight for survival, and rebranding to moderate success in the 1980s.

Kiss parted ways with Glickman-Marks in 1988, and soon afterward, with his experience "at the front of my brain," Chris decided to put pen to paper and create a memoir. The resulting *Kiss and Sell* initially did not sell, but in the wake of the band's 1996 reunion success, Billboard Books published it. It has since become recognized as a landmark tome, not only with Kiss fans, who appreciate its hyperbole-free candor (something of a rarity in the Kiss world), but also as a solid resource pertaining to the 1970's music biz in general — and somewhat comedically — an exploration of rock-star egos.

Chris wasn't super-involved in the production of *Kiss Meets The Phantom of The Park*, but his recollections from his then-vantage point help to outline some of the inner workings of Kiss, circa 1978.

Ron: First off, *Kiss and Sell* is my favorite KISS book.

Christopher Lendt: Thank you. I spent a lot of time on it. I wanted it to be something I could be personally proud of, as well as tell the story of KISS, from my perspective. I researched it carefully, and confirmed my recollections. It's also an insider's view of what the music business is like, which is something I think very few people know about.

Ron: That's the thing — you don't have to be a superfan of the band to enjoy it.

Chris: That's what I was aiming at: I wanted it to be appreciated on two levels. First of all, as an insider's account of what the Kiss story was all about, and secondly, the music business. Regardless if Kiss is or isn't someone's favorite band.

Ron: I've been a Kiss fan through thick and thin; I bought *Animalize* the day it came out!

Chris: They are a lot of stalwarts, that I think were well rewarded by the band. They have also allowed Kiss to go out in a grand style, that none of us dreamed was possible ten years ago.

Ron: After the book, have you heard from Gene or Paul personally?

Chris: No.

Ron: Did you hear anything through the grapevine?

Chris: Only the most sketchy and incomplete details. I've never heard anything very critical, but I've seen a few mentions of the book by them in magazines. Paul said that although he did not agree with everything in the book — and I certainly wouldn't expect that he would — he said it was a credible and respectable job. It was kind of feint praise, but from Paul, more than one was likely to expect *(laughs)*. So nothing directly from them, and they did not go out of their way to talk about the book. It would be absurd to attack it for credibility, because I probably have more credibility than probably anybody that has written a book about a musical artist from an insider's view up to this point — or I am certainly one of them. So I don't think that would have been a very smart tack for them. At the same time, a lot of what I talk about is stuff that they would have been happy if the world did notknow about it! Not that I think that there is anything detrimental, or damaging, or in any way negative about the band.

> **"I had a wonderful 12-year experience – the experience of a lifetime."**

I had a wonderful 12-year experience — the experience of a lifetime. But their point of view is different than mine. They're protective of their image; they only want politically correct, officially approved events to be known to the public. While I understand that, it was not my objective. I tried to present a very balanced picture, the pros and cons, the pluses and minuses, the peaks and the valleys. And I think their fans are perhaps are little more mature than they give them credit for. I think only a very young and immature fan would pick up my book and say, "I don't believe it — Kiss are gods from another universe." Of course, they have some fans like that, every band does, but as soon as they get past junior high age, as clearly most of them are today, I think they see it's a band like Aerosmith, or the Rolling Stones — they have a history. Everybody wasn't always buddy-buddy. They had a lot of personal problems, just like every band that you read about. I think that Kiss wanted to kind of maintain a saintly — maybe that's the wrong word — a kind of *glorified* image, and in this day and age, I don't think that really holds up that well. What I hope that fans get out of the book is that this is the *real* Kiss. They had a lot of good points, they're tremendous performers, I enjoyed working with them a great deal, and they also had their problems, like every band.

Ron: Something I liked about the book, and I'm not sure you did it intentionally, was the use of deadpan humor.

Chris: I'm delighted you picked that up. A lot of stuff, I thought was funny. Not in a slapstick way, but in terms of the personalities and incongruities of a bunch of guys like Kiss, who are four *totally* different personalities. And a lot of the guys they dealt with on the business side were also characters in their own right. To me, it had all the makings of a great movie, with tremendously larger-than-life characters.

Ron: Paul Stanley didn't need a decorator; he needed "a super decorator"!

Chris: Yeah *(laughs)*. For every band read you read about, there are a thousand artists who act and behave in the same way. A lot of what goes on is driven by egos. In the '70s the ego manifested itself in different ways.

Ron: Have you made any headway with making this required reading in any universities?

Chris: I have done mailings to several hundred universities where I know they teach a college course in the music business. I have appeared on panels at conferences, and done interviews all over the country. The book is being read already in some universities.

Ron: Basically, my approach writing about *Kiss Meets The Phantom* is like yours; I want to create something with a wide appeal — to pop culture fans, people into the '70s, Hanna-Barbera, and of course, Kiss. Do you remember when you first heard talk of there being a Kiss movie?

Chris: There had always been talk in the inner circle — and of course, that included Bill Aucoin at the time — that Kiss was perfect for a film, or a cartoon series.

Ron: I spoke to Bill recently. I asked him where *his* book is!

Chris: Good idea! I take great pleasure in saying this: Bill Aucoin was probably the most talented and creatively gifted person that I have met in the music business. He was one of the rare people who had a real touch with artists. Whenever I was in a room with him, they gravitated toward him, he was sensitive to them, was able to communicate with them, and they really liked being around him. He really had a knack, and was a visionary. Did he mention my book?

> "It was important to do the movie, and make it look like a Kiss vehicle."

Ron: I did, and he didn't discredit it.

Chris: I would have been surprised if he did. That's what I would expect. But one thing you discover when doing an insider book is that everyone has their point of view.

Ron: About the cartoon idea: do you know if any art was made, as a proof of concept?

Chris: To the best of my knowledge, no. But, I would not be the last word on that. I would only be involved once something like that would come to fruition. I was only involved on the business end, not creative.

Ron: Along that line, do you recall how much Kiss was paid for doing the movie?

Chris: My recollection is somewhere in the neighborhood of $50,000. At that time, TV movies were not paying huge sums. Second, the budget of the movie was quite high due to the special effects, and locations — shooting at Magic Mountain. I'm sure it wasn't a priority of Bill's or Kiss, that they got the most amount of money to do a movie. It was important to do the movie, and make it look like a Kiss vehicle.

Ron: How did Kiss first land on TV, rather than a movie screen?

Chris: I only remember there was a relationship with NBC. At that time, Al Ross was employed by Bill, as an executive. He had developed something called the *Rock and Roll Olympics*, only you couldn't call it that, because "Olympics" was trademarked. So they changed it to *Rock and Roll Sports Classic*, and apparently that was a program that NBC bought. They developed a relationship with NBC, and one thing led to another. Kiss was the hottest group in the world then, and they *(Aucoin and Ross)* had the idea. I had no involvement with that deal. I only dealt with it after it became a reality, and then it became a matter of organization and attending to details.

Ron: Speaking of which, in your book you talk about scripts, abut there being draft after draft. One of the scriptwriters talked about one of the meetings being a showdown between Kiss members regarding who had the highest number of lines.

Chris: It's possible!

Ron: Did you ever hear anything about Kiss being offered a role in *Sgt. Pepper's Lonely Hearts Club Band*?

Chris: That I never heard. That would be news to me.

Ron: You stayed with the band when they were in based in Los Angeles during shooting, right?

Chris: Yes. All of the band members were at L'Ermitage *(a hotel in Beverly Hills)*.

Ron: Did you visit the movie set?

Chris: I remember going a few times.

Ron: Do you remember tales of drama and/or craziness on the set?

Chris: Oh, sure. Like I mention in my book, Peter would show up completely exhausted from the night before. Ace had similar ... *limitations*. They would be out all night, and these films start shooting at five, six a.m. They would be tired, and ornery. It was just very difficult. First of all, Peter and Ace weren't really into being in a TV movie. Second, there were their states of mind at that time; they were not exactly conducive to that hard work regimen.

Ron: Do you think their attitudes at the time were due to their workload up to that point, or just their personalities?

Chris: It was a combination. They had just finished some touring, and had a very busy schedule. Then, they went out and did this movie, and keep in mind that nobody in Kiss had prior experience as actors. That was a big unknown factor; it wasn't like they were going to do a movie about Kiss in concert, or even backstage. They were going to actually *act in a movie*. It didn't matter if they were going to do one that appealed to 8 year olds, or 28-year olds — you still have to act. You have to be trained, and you still have to deliver lines. It's very hard to cover up. It was quite an ambitious undertaking to get them to try and do what the Beatles did in *A Hard Day's Night*, which was to assume the role of actors, and do it in a way that was credible.

Ron: What the vibe around the Glickman-Marks offices about this venture?

Chris: Howard Marks would have been the closest to what was going on, and he must have been enthusiastic about it. He saw himself as a big promoter and marketing person. He was also a big booster of Bill at the time, so these kinds of plans — to have Kiss in a movie on NBC TV — was a huge promotional bonanza. I'm sure he was in lockstep behind Bill in trying to make it happen.

Ron: So, Ace and Peter were not into it, but Gene was into it enough for all three of them!

Chris: I'm sure Gene was delighted to play the character he portrayed on stage, in a different media. He was certainly a very disciplined person, he always has been. Peter and Ace were much more faithful to the rock and roll lifestyle.

Ron: And yet, at the time, Peter was saying in interviews, "I want to be the next Al Pacino."

Chris *(laughing)***:** That's right!

Ron: And, as well as being an avowed Sinatra-phile, you would think he would have given it his all.

Chris: Well, Peter at that time — and I'm being charitable here — had kind of had a romanticized image of Frank Sinatra. Peter was mesmerized by the imagery of Sinatra — that easy style, having a perfect way with words, being a man's man, with a rough charm. That's what Peter was in love with. The real work that it took to become Sinatra, as an actor, a song stylist, and performer? I don't think Peter really thought it through that much!

Ron: Peter's voice in the film was eventually overdubbed, and according to voice actor Michael Bell, who ended up doing it, it was because he had a lisp. Did you hear anything like that?

Chris: A lisp? If you ask me, Peter was overdubbed because he is not terribly articulate. He didn't enunciate well. His voice was kind of mumbled. It had to do with the fact that he was frequently exhausted, in a depressed state of mind, and his words just came out kind of garbled.

Ron: He had a tough-guy voice, but a lethargic tough-guy voice.

Chris: Exactly.

Ron: I don't think it would have sounded right for a feline superhero. Funny enough, with the overdubbing, I think Peter comes off as the best Kiss actor in the movie!

Chris: Could be.

Ron: When was the first time you saw the film?

Chris: There was a party in a private screening room, with people from ATI and Aucoin Management. I also remember seeing it on TV the night it was shown.

Ron: There was that press conference at Magic Mountain.

Chris: I remember being there during filming and meeting Leif Erikson.

Ron: Erikson? Oh, Leif *Garrett?*

Chris: Yes, that's it. I'm sorry — I have an Ericsson telephone! Yeah — he was at the show with a very good looking woman. I also remember seeing Kiss perform. There was a lot of set up for that.

Ron: Speaking of good-looking women, there is a nice photo from Kiss' 1980 Australia tour in *Kiss and Sell.*

Chris: Right — I made sure they put that one in!

Ron: It looks like you had a terrible time that night.

Chris: Yes.

Ron: Did you ever attend any *Attack of The Phantoms* screenings while overseas?

Chris: The only premiere I recall going to was in Australia was *Superman II*. It was actually released there before it was in the United States, and we happened to be there, and got to go to a screening.

Ron: Legend has it that the Hanna-Barbera press clippings book for *Kiss Meets ...* contains just one — out of hundreds — positive review. Do you recall hearing anything reaction wise among the band members after the project was done and aired?

Chris: It was pretty much on the same wavelength after, as during, filming. They thought they all looked bad. I remember Paul saying, "we've just proved that none of us are actors." Who came off the least bad? That's a matter of opinion. It was something they cringed at.

> "It was something they cringed at."

Ron: Paul is particularly stilted in the film.

Chris: The character in the movie was nothing like Paul on stage! The stage Paul is high-energy, rock and roll. The part he played in the movie had nothing to do with that.

Ron: I think the movie did a lot to sow the seeds of a successful reunion in 1996; I think it did succeed in expanding the Kiss audience, but the band couldn't really tap into it until the '90s.

Chris: I don't know that the movie was such an icon of popular culture — I think you're stretching it! To diehard Kiss fans, it was very important, but I don't think it went beyond that.

Ron: In the aftermath of the movie, Gene was running around in the press, saying there would be a theatrical feature in 1979, complete with it own soundtrack album. Do you recall hearing about any of those plans?

Chris: No. He says a lot of things, that are based more on hype, because that is what his jobs is. So what he would do is take anything that was talked about three steps further, and make it sort of a pre-announcement. There were a lot of things talked about, but as the group's popularity waned after 1979, a lot of people passed on those things.

Think of the three main behind-the-scenes branches of the '70s Kiss tree as being Aucoin Management, Casablanca Records, and Glickman-Marks management, with the latter being Chris' place of perch.

PHANTOM FINDINGS
Ducking Away from My Work

There I was, working on this thing in my favorite coffee shop (or at least one of them). It was like any other writing day, except I was a bit tired, and my mind was wandering. A young lady is sitting next to me, and I see that she too is writing. I ask her what she is working on.

"Oh, I am doing my thesis, on 'submerged aquatic vegetation and water quality as drivers of waterfowl abundance in Back Bay, Virginia.'" She adds that she "attends university" abroad, in London. Looking in the direction of my laptop, she asks what I am up to.

"Uh, I am writing a book related to the 1978 TV Movie starring the rock group Kiss, called *Kiss Meets The Phantom of The Park*." I then deftly angle my computer away from her line of sight a bit, so she cannot see my Google page full of "Kiss on cubes" shots.

The gal looks at me politely, but blankly, and says, "I was born in 1995." Hmmm ... ducks were around a lot longer than Kiss!

Most people are kind of intrigued, if not impressed by my project, but here, I was dead in the water. Thinking fast, I ask her if she has interviewed any ducks from Back Bay for her paper. She cracks (quacks) up, and I return to working.

James Hulsey
Art Director
Interview conducted March 10, 2002

Talk about hiring the right person for the job! By 1978, James was not only a veteran of art direction in the TV industry, but he also had a specifically perfect pedigree for a Kiss project — working on things like an Evel Knievel movie and episodes of *Wonder Woman* and *The Amazing Spider-Man* saw him super-ready to give *Kiss Meets The Phantom of The Park* a similarly colorful, live-action comic book look.

And, he nailed it. His work has had this author rewinding, pausing, and zooming in for decades. Abner's laboratory, the Chamber of Thrills, and Kiss' mansion headquarters were all made under his charge, and man, what awesomeness.

Interview background: I first made contact with James while sitting in a crowded and noisy fast food place on Magic Mountain Parkway, after being in "the park" all day *(I think it was a Carl's Jr.)*. We planned to speak upon my returning to New Jersey, and did so soon after.

James Hulsey: What is it you'd like to know?

Ron: Basically, anything you could say about your work on *Kiss Meets ...* would be great for me. I have some questions that may jog your memory. For starters, what exactly is an "art director"?

James: An art director is someone who gets a script, and breaks it down, scene by scene, and determines what has to be built, designed, and found on location. You combine all those things, and then you sit down and design the look of the picture, and then present it to the producer, director ... whoever is the most powerful *(laughs)*. Then, after designing the sets, you see to the building of them, decorating of them, and dressing of them. Also, depending on the confidence the director has in you, you tell them how it is supposed to be shot. Some directors hate that — they don't want to be told what to do.

Ron: So, you created the visual style of *Kiss Meets The Phantom of The Park.*

> *"I drew something up, and said, 'Make this thing look like a snake.'"*

Jim: That's right.

Ron: Fascinating.

Jim: Well, at lot of people say that we are responsible for everything that is out of focus behind the actor!

Ron: Right!

Jim: For example, that laboratory was all on stage.

Ron: That was at Culver City, correct?

Jim: Yes. Well, first on location at Magic Mountain, when people go to a corner where people supposedly go to enter the lab, I built that entrance — it did not exist. And when they passed through that, the entrance was on location, and of course the elevator and lab were on stage.

Ron: That lab set is a big favorite. I also love it because it seems to evoke a bit of the original *Star Trek*.

Jim: The so-called Chamber of Horrors was on another stage, with those actors, who were moving very ... jerkily, not like automatons *(laughs)*.

Ron: How much of the lab set was built from the ground up?

Jim: Everything was built, except for a lot of the computer-like stuff, which was rented from a special effects shop. We built the elevator, and that console, where he *(Abner)* moves back and forth, like a gun turret —

Ron: — with the primitive Sony monitors.

Jim: That house where Kiss supposedly lived, or stayed, was up in the hills above Culver City, and was originally owned by the man who perfected the altimeter for aircraft *(Paul Kollsman)*. It was empty, and at that time rented out to movie companies. I just took an empty room, and created that Kiss-like area, with the crazy plants, and snake couch.

Ron: The snake couch!

Jim (laughing): We built that snake couch. We made it in the prop shop.

Ron: Did you just envision a snake couch, and then told them to make it?

Jim: Right. I drew something up, and said, "Make this thing look like a snake."

Ron: Wow — what does *your* house look like?

Jim: Well, I live in a small house, and don't bring that stuff home with me!

Ron: Where do you think the snake couch is today?

Jim: Oh, God — I'm sure it's long since gone. Maybe somebody got it. Once a show or film is finished, you either trash everything, destroy it, or send back stuff to rental houses.

Ron: Do you recall any of the names of the rental places?

Jim: I think some of the computer stuff came from a guy name Woody. That was so long ago.

Ron: How did you get the gig?

Jim: I worked show by show, and Terry *(Morse)* and I had worked together on three or four shows. Maybe that's how I got it. That was actually Hanna-Barbera, right?

Ron: Yes, it was co-produced by them. I was wondering if you used any of their stuff.

Jim: No. They *(HB)* would just turn over everything to the producer.

Ron: I did notice in the lab set, there are a couple of costume heads of Hanna-Barbera characters. Maybe there were stuck in there as an in-joke or something?

Jim: I'll have to look.

(One head is "Hair Bear," from Help! … it's the Hair Bear Bunch — see more "bunch" below. The other is "Fleegle," from The Banana Splits. Ironically, at the time of filming, Magic Mountain had their own characters that were really cool. In the theatrical cut of the movie, their troll-like "Bloop" can be seen interacting with park attendees early on. Incidentally, these shots seem to be "real," and not shots of extras pretending to be having fun with the furry mascots, or rather, having their hat stolen by one. With the advent of Six Flags buying Magic Mountain in 1979 or so, the characters were eventually phased out for Warner Brothers properties. Nonetheless, the likes of Bleep, Bloop, and the Wizard live on in MM fans' memories, and auctions on eBay, where this author has acquired some park merchandise branded with them).

> *"... those guys were not actors! They were very hard to control."*

Ron: And, what's more, and this may be getting a little too obscure, that same head or something close to it was in an episode of the *Brady Bunch* — Greg wore it! (*That's the more "bunch" mentioned earlier.*)

Jim: I might have picked it up and threw it in there.

Ron: The lab set was pretty big.

Jim: It filled up a small stage. It was maybe 80 by 100 feet. They had separate rooms, where the big door slid open, and he (*Abner*) had a secret chamber within the lab. All that metal looking stuff was not really metal — it was metal Formica, glued to plywood.

Ron: How did you feel about the scenery at Magic Mountain? Was there anything that you felt needed to be changed?

Jim: Actually, there were a number of things.

Ron: There was some Kiss art put around near the entrance.

Jim: Yeah. I had those pedestals built. And then, all the stuff, when he walks through the wall at night — that was actually the back lot at the studio.

Ron: All the rides were definitely at Magic Mountain, right?

Jim: All at Magic Mountain.

Ron: So, you set up a wall on a back lot.

Jim: They wouldn't let us do that at Magic Mountain. We probably only shot at Magic Mountain two nights, and then we did backgrounds of the roller coaster so we could put Kiss in.

Ron: I spoke to Gordon Hessler, and that opening sequence has nighttime shots of the rides and then black screen shots of the band, superimposed over them. How much would you have worked on something like that?

Jim: I had to be on the stage, and my construction people had to build shapes and boxes so Kiss could walk and sit on them, and then paint them blue, so they would disappear. Like when they are walking across the waterfall. I am there as a consultant to the director.

Ron: So, you built the stuff for them to "walk" over that waterfall?

Jim: Yes.

Ron: If you look closely, you'll see Gene sort of nervously step through that. His boots were not made for that.

Jim: And those guys were not actors! They were very hard to control, really. Gene was the most cooperative. One of the others —

Ron: — Paul Stanley? The "Starchild"?

Jim: No, he was okay ... who was another guy?

Ron: Ace Frehley, "Space Ace"?

Jim: He was — to be quite honest with you — quite loaded most of the time. When you make a movie, you do a little piece, one line, or one speech, and then the so-called actor has to go sit down and wait. He didn't like that, and he got on a motor scooter, and drove out of the studio with a bottle of champagne, and almost got hit by a car. I think at that point, but I'm not too sure, I think the group was kind of falling apart.

Ron: Did you glean that from being on the set?

Jim: Yeah. There was too much dissension — you could tell. And they had handlers, always hanging around. They were also still trying to project the image that they would never be seen without their makeup. They were anonymous people, and I think some didn't like that. There was tension, you could tell. And they were *not* cooperative with the director!

Ron: Did you see them without makeup back then?

Jim: Never.

Ron: At this point in your career, you were quite experienced.

Jim: Oh, yes, I did 70 shows.

Ron: Including an *Amazing Spider-Man* TV series credit.

Jim: You saw that? I also did *Wonder Woman*. Lynda Carter, beautiful woman, not much of an actress *(laughs)*.

Ron: I'm thinking your work on superhero productions was a catalyst in Terry Morse recruiting you.

> "She was really not an actress, the poor thing."

Jim: Terry and I did a thing called *Throwdown*, a cop thriller, and then he and I did something about a Korean detective. It was a cute story, but it never went any place. It was also for Hanna-Barbera. He did a lot for them.

Ron: What did you think of the Kiss movie then, and what do you think of it now?

Jim: Well, it's pretty dated, and the acting is pretty terrible. It's really interesting that years after I did that, I was on a scout *(looking at locations)* in Paris, walking around, and saw the movie's poster! It was so bad, I thought, *how could they like it?* Anthony Zerbe was okay, I mean he was pretty good.

Ron: Yes, I agree.

Jim: The girl *(Deborah Ryan)* was terrible, and the young boy *(Terry Lester)* was awful. They were really not actors. She was like non-existent. Is she still around?

Ron: I have been trying to interview her for years. Terry actually gave me a lead on her. I am not sure if it was a case of his just sticking her in the movie.

Jim: She was *really* not an actress, the poor thing.

Ron: And, she was playing up against Anthony Zerbe. Carmine Caridi also put in a good performance. He was the owner of the park.

Jim: Oh yeah — he was *okay (thinking, as if wanting to take back his "okay" description)* he was a little, uh …*(cracks up)*.

I must say, Gordon Hessler was the sweetest guy in the world, and we read the script, and we said, "What is this about?" We couldn't figure it out. It was like, "Let's just do it the way we want to!"

Ron: Did you know that originally there was another "Sam"? It was Sam Cotton.

Jim: Yeah, I remember that. There was a controversy.

Ron: I heard they filmed for at least a couple of days before they replaced him.

Jim: If they did, I didn't know it. But I'm not always on the set.

Ron: Did you have anything to do with the drawing of the storyboards?

Jim: I think some of those came out of Hanna-Barbera. We really didn't follow them too much, I must say.

Ron: Here's something that I am not sure would have fallen under your purview: there's a scene with Zerbe and Caridi where they are walking among those Kiss art things you guys put up, in the front of the park. There's a plane that flies overhead, that advertises the Kiss show with a streaming banner.

Jim: We did that. We called an aerial display company, and they towed a Kiss banner.

Ron: Would you happen to recall the name of that company?

Jim: Uh ... I couldn't remember if my life depended on it. We used to have a book of people, suppliers.

Ron: Was the Chamber of Thrills set also built from scratch?

Jim: Every bit, yes.

Ron: That was a two-room set?

Jim: It was kind of like a half-circle, so the camera could follow. It's so interesting that somebody got into this ... how *did* you get into this? *(Ron explains his whole Kiss movie fascination)* An interesting side note was that Gene was going with Cher. She was on the set the night we did the scene where he walked through the wall, and crashed through the concession stand. The big shadow on the wall, with the two guards, who were not very good actors. Maybe it was done intentionally, but I don't think so!

Ron: One of the guards was Brion James, who went on to do some other stuff.

Jim: Yeah — he played a heavy in a lot of stuff.

Ron: I always wondered about product placement in this film. Was there any?

Jim: No. At the time, it was frowned upon. Something to do with the FCC.

> "Somebody from the product affairs department probably saw it, and we had to black it out."

Ron: There seems to be a lot of it. For example, when Deveraux is at his turret, and looking at his monitors, the Sony logo is clearly seen. Later on, it's gone! Did you have a continuity person on set?

Jim: No. Somebody from the product affairs department probably saw it, and we had to black it out.

Ron: Even when Gene destroys the concession stand, there are like 1,000 Coca-Cola logos, on cups and stuff.

Jim: Purely by accident.

Ron: Even when Sam goes to shoot photos of Kiss, there's a close-up of a Nikon camera — it's like an advertisement for them: "takes great photos to design robots from!"

Jim: The studios were deaf on that *(product placement)*. Hanna-Barbera was an independent company, so maybe they let all that go by.

Ron: There are a few additional scenes in the overseas theatrical version. It all makes for kind of a better film, actually *(2002 opinion alert)*.

Jim: Maybe that's why the French liked it!

Ron: There is one where Melissa is walking out to the lot — this is after Sam has been abducted — and she is checking on his car. It's a yellow Volkswagen "Bug" *(Beetle)*. Did you have to get that car for that scene?

Jim: Yes, right. It was probably one of the crew members' cars.

Ron: Did you ever go as far as doing wardrobe?

Jim: It depends.

Ron: Carmine Caridi said he wore some of his own clothes.

Jim: He probably did. It was a low-budget thing.

Ron: Did you have anything to do with the scene of the creatures on the roller coaster?

Jim: The stuntmen were brought in, and the director and I said they should be big, white monkeys. It was off-the-rack stuff.

Ron: Deke Heyward was upset that they had whiskers.

Ron: What did you think of Kiss' music?

Jim: It was very exciting. In concert, with the effects, and the smoke ... you heard a little of it, and that was enough *(laughs)*!

Ron: The concert at Magic Mountain on May 19 was filmed.

Jim: How that happened was the studio put on a free concert. We wanted a big crowd.

Ron: And then the band returned to the stage the next day to do pickups, and fight their doubles.

Jim: Yeah.

Ron: And there was a supposedly a scene where one of the guys would be throwing roses at the camera, a P.O.V. thing.

Jim: I don't know.

Ron: Did you speak with Gene Simmons on set?

Jim: Not really. Except for the blue screen stuff, where they were flying through the air, and stepping on pedestals.

Ron: Did they have to do numerous takes of walking on the pedestals?

Jim: Oh, yes, we spent almost a day and a night there. It was a very slow process.

Ron: You mentioned flying – they show the guys sitting in —

Jim: — bumper cars. We took it from Magic Mountain, hung it with wires above the stage. Again, all against a blue screen. We later rotoscoped the wires out.

Ron: In the very beginning of the movie, there is a Kiss image that spins in. How was that done?

Jim: That was done in post-production. They take the image, and put it in an optical printer. The poster was about 2 feet square.

Ron: Do you recall setting up the marching band?

Jim: I think Terry did that. I didn't have anything to do with it.

Ron: How long did you work on *Kiss Meets ...* in total?

Jim: Pre-production time is usually about a month on something like that. And then shooting was about 21 days. My main contact was Gordon, who has to talk to the production company, or whoever's complaining!

Ron: Did you have to fill the pool with water?

Jim: No, the house was used quite often by movie companies. The guy that owned it had a plan to develop houses there. There were models in the garage.

Ron: How much were you paid for your work?

Jim: At that time, I was making about $1,000 a week. I was free-lance. At that time, the studio system was coming apart, and you went from job to job.

Ron: When you see the finished product on screen, is there anything in particular that you think looks great?

Jim: I like the lab.

Ron: I wish we saw more of it.

Jim: I do, too.

Ron: Did you go to any of the premiere parties?

Jim: Yes, I went to the first one.

Ron: Is *Kiss Meets The Phantom of The Park* the greatest thing you have ever worked on?

Jim: Well, it was fun, but my crowning achievement is *A Streetcar Name Desire*, with Ann Margaret. I got an Emmy for that. Also *The Letter (1982 TV movie)* and *An Early Frost (1985 TV movie)*.

Barry Levine
On-set photographer
Interview conducted March 5, 2001

Barry Levine has done some of the greatest Kiss photo sessions, ever. Right from the first time they got him, he *got them*. His shoots were as creative, varied, and dynamic as the band itself — backgrounds ranged from "homemade" glitter ones, to Mylar (*yes, that is a brand name*), and even New York City itself, in the group's famed shoot atop the Empire State Building. In the foreground, his work is filled not only with an expressive, in-character Kiss, but also the occasional prop. That crazy and cool list includes oh, a Colonial American flag (*part of a wicked "Spirit of '76" take*), a medieval weapon (*yes, the "Demon" Gene Simmons brandished it*), motorcycles (*choppers!*), strobe lights (*I never knew they could be that cool*), and live animals ("*Catman" Peter Criss posed with two panthers in 1978!*). That's not all; acrylic was pressed into various forms and service, such as lightsaber-like tubes the band brandished (*at least that is what they looked like, to this then 8-year old*), chairs (*Ace sat in one, almost Captain Kirk-like*), and cube-shaped pedestals.

All of his Kiss work is amazing, but it is the 1977 series of photos colloquially known as the "cubes session" (utilizing the aforementioned pedestals, with Kiss atop them) that at least for a while were their most famous, if not solely most ubiquitous. Beyond appearing in poster (*find that Canadian one!*) and pinup form, these were the shots that adorned myriad Kiss products, such as the *Kiss Your Face* makeup kit (*"by Remco, yeah!"*), Mego's awesome Kiss dolls (*"they look insane!"*), and the Kiss Colorforms play set, which in this writer's estimation features the #2 original Kiss villain of all time, "The Mad Rock Promoter."

Given his history (*Kissstory*) with the group, it is unsurprising that Barry was brought aboard to photograph Kiss' TV movie making. His work captured both the excitement and disillusion the group were experiencing. Also detectable is some of the general weariness various group members were going through. The best stuff may be the stills of the band members posing on the sets between takes; Gene in particular put in one of his best shoots ever on the Chamber of Thrills set, being a demon in a horror movie candy store.

My *Kiss Meets* ... mission amused Barry, and to put it another way, he *broke my balls* a bit about it! He was also supportive. While transcribing his interview, it was a surprise remembrance to hear that at the time, he was serving as a go-between between myself, and none other than Gene Simmons, talking up this project.

We talked a few times *(he once called me from a dentist's chair — that was a short convo)*, but only one cassette (roll of audio film?) has been located. On it, we *frame* Barry's pre-Kiss camera career, leading into his days with the fearsome foursome, and of course his Kiss movie memories. At one point, Barry describes his younger self as having been arrogant, and someone who partook in some mind-altering partying here and there. As such, when being pressed about movie minutiae, he eventually exclaims in a surrendering fashion, "That was a long time ago; I'm lucky I can remember the '80s!"

By 2001, Barry felt he was almost "completely opposite" from his old self, and on the *(platform)* heels of working with Gene in producing the 1999 Kiss movie *Detroit Rock City (it's no Kiss Meets ...*), he was looking forward to doing more projects with the Demon.

Now, let's bring his interview into *focus*.

Barry Levine: Are you there?

Ron: Yeah.

Barry *(in a mock tone of woeful resignation)*: Oh, Jesus! Anyway, what's happening? I talked to Gene today, and he said he would think about it *(about this book project)* while he's overseas. He says he can help manipulate it, and when he gets back, he would be happy to talk to you.

Ron: Great! Barry, even as a kid, I always knew who you were, as I always intently studied every single printed word about Kiss.

Barry: People consider me the guy who took all the best pictures of them. And, I have shot all kinds of groups, but they were the best group to shoot, because they were the most theatrical.

Ron: Back in 1978, what were you doing project wise when the call came from the Kiss offices to shoot on the set of the movie?

> **"I was Paul's best friend at the time. He was the guy I was tightest with."**

Barry: I was working Queen and Abba. I had just gotten back from Sweden. They (Abba) had flown me over there.

Ron: You shot an Abba cover, right?

Barry: The one with the four drawings on the front, there's actually a shot inside, of them on top of a building. They used my stuff for all kinds of posters and everything.

Ron: They flew you over, huh?

Barry: Yeah. I got so much money for doing that it was ridiculous. They were great people.

Ron: By the time Kiss first hit the scene, would you say you were you fully established in your photography career?

Barry: I was established in England. I had shot The Clash, Generation X, the Boomtown Rats, and the Sex Pistols.

Ron: Wow, that is a good chunk of the '70s English punk scene!

Barry: Yeah, everybody. The first band I ever shot over there was The Sweet. I did their cover for "Sweet F.A." *(this may have been for their single of "Action," where "Sweet F.A." was the B-side)*. Here, I was up and coming. I had shot everybody — the New York Dolls, all kinds of people. Tina Turner. But I really got established with Kiss.

Ron: So, you had dipped into the earlier glam on both sides of the Atlantic, too.

Barry: Yeah, glam, punk, pop — all that stuff.

Ron: Prior to *Kiss Meets* ... did you do a lot of on-set movie photography?

Barry: That was my first movie shooting stills. And being their photographer — as opposed to being a photographer hired by NBC — I could do whatever I wanted, shoot whenever I wanted.

Ron: So, you were there in a "Kiss staffer" capacity?

Barry: Yes. I would shoot between takes, backstage, everything. I would be on the set all the time.

Ron: How many rolls of film did you go through?

Barry: I would say probably about 200 rolls.

Ron: Did you use one camera at a time, or have more than one, as to not miss anything?

Barry: Yeah, I would always have about two or three cameras on me.

Ron: Did you shoot anything during *Kiss Meets* ... in black and white?

Barry: Most of the time when I shot Kiss, I'd say 99.9 percent of the time, I shot color. I never wanted to shoot black and white. I told them that if they wanted black and white, they would have to get another photographer *(laughs)*. I knew at the time that nobody could do what I was doing with that kind of photography, doing these sets, effects, and lighting. People were just doing these gray backgrounds and things like that.

> **"I thought it was going to be a little cooler."**

Ron: I have always loved the Kiss shoot where the band was on the cubes.

Barry: Oh, God — I hated that! That sucks.

Ron: *You didn't like that?*

Barry: Everything else that came out of the session I like: the Mylar background, and other stuff. But them, on the cubes, to me, was the most embarrassing shooting I have ever done in my life.

Ron: Why?

Barry: Nothing came out like I wanted to, but everyone was like, "This is cool!"

Ron: Whose idea was it to use the cubes?

Barry: Every idea was mine. I would come in with all the designs, and they would say yes or no.

Ron: So, about that shoot, in your head you had one idea of how things would look, and then the execution and final product wasn't quite the same?

Barry: Yeah. I had done something like that before, but on a bigger scale, with Jane Seymour. She was on a big chair made of plexiglass, and [it was] lit. It was filled with smoke, and you couldn't see any edges of the chair. My favorite Kiss session was the sparkle background one, where they were holding the light balls.

Ron: Were those lights in that shoot battery powered?

Barry: No, they were just regular hanging light fixtures. I put a strobe in them, and the more light you gave them, the more of a different shape they would take. Everything I did, I did in the camera. I didn't believe in airbrushing. It was all what you saw. We hid the wires in their sleeves. A lot of people thought the Empire State Building photo was an airbrushed one.

Ron: It seems you really enjoyed the creative opportunities that working with Kiss provided.

Barry: Of course. I wanted to make money, but Kiss has always given me carte blanche. I did the two sessions when they first came back. The first one we did was great, with the barbed wire around Gene's head (this was in 1996, during the band's original-member reunion era that lasted until 2001).

> "When they weren't filming, I would grab them and shoot."

Ron: He also held a kimono dragon in that shoot.

Barry: That was one of my best sessions.

40   *Conversations with Phantoms*

Ron: What did you think of the visual look of *Kiss Meets The Phantom of The Park*?

Barry: I thought it was very cool. I also thought that as far as Kiss as actors, it was fucking ridiculous! I told Gene and Paul: "This is dumb." I was laughing; I thought it was very funny. When they weren't filming, I would grab them and shoot — Gene coming out of the casket in the dungeon. I was able to light the sets myself. I brought my own lights, and re-lit them.

> "Kiss has always given me carte blanche."

Ron: How were the movie guys, with regard to you hanging around the set?

Barry: I really never gave a shit, because I was an arrogant, little f*ck. I wasn't the nicest guy at times, in those days.

Ron: I ask because I am hearing that Gordon Hessler ran a tight set.

Barry: He was pretty arrogant, but I was Kiss' photographer, and more than that, I was Paul's best friend at the time. He was the guy I was tightest with.

Ron: Since you were close, did he ever pull you aside during filming, and say, "I'm suffering here"?

Barry: He was very self-effacing, and would just laugh. He didn't think he was dong Shakespeare.

Ron: How did Gene feel about the movie?

Barry: Gene thought it was kind of cool, and thought it would catch on, as a novelty thing. He didn't realize what they were doing was unadulterated shit.

Ron: How about Ace and Peter?

Barry: Oh, they could f*cking care less. They didn't know where they *were*, never mind what they were doing.

Ron: Peter, in particular?

Barry: He was out of his mind in those days.

Ron: The band was pretty much exhausted at that point.

Barry: I think it [the movie] hurt them a bit. I think it hurt their relationship with Bill Aucoin, too.

Ron: He was sort of a major catalyst behind the project.

Barry: Yeah. They blamed him for everything.

Ron: Did you try to sneak into a crowd scene during filming, maybe to try and do a cameo?

Barry: Nah.

Ron: Who was the best actor in the band?

Barry: Gene. He is a good actor.

Ron: Did you catch on to the camp nature of the project right away?

Barry: I thought it was going to be a little cooler.

Ron: The scriptwriters are pretty much retired from writing.

Barry: I'd be retired, if I wrote that script. The best thing about the whole thing was the concert footage.

Ron: You shot that, right?

Barry: Yes, it really was the best thing, out of everything.

Ron: Did you go to the premiere?

Barry: Yes.

Ron: Did you bring a camera with you?

Barry: No. I would never do that kind of stuff. I spent so much time with them, and I wouldn't take a camera with me into a lot of places, that I maybe should have. I just wasn't into doing that.

Jan-Michael Sherman
Co-Scriptwriter
Interview conducted February 2, 2001

One of the first items on your author's bucket list with this project was to interview the scriptwriters. That is where it all starts from, right? In its various incarnations *(written, revised, and filmed)* Kiss Meets The Phantom of The Park is a serviceable, mild horror and science fiction fantasy story. It is also laced with some clever dialogue and memorable wacky lingo *(hang out with some Kiss fans for a while, and you are bound to hear some of it)*. In short, these guys (*Jan-Michael Sherman and Don Buday*) pretty much came up with what needed to be come up with.

Jan-Michael was excited to talk about his contribution to the Kiss world, and in 2001 he was seemingly just as enthusiastic about it as he was in 1978.

Jan-Micheal Sherman: So, you're in Jersey?

Ron: Yes — Hoboken.

Jan-Michael: I was born in Brooklyn! But this is your nickel. You tracked me down — I don't know how you did this! My wife told me that you're writing a book?

Ron: Yes, on the classic TV movie, Kiss Meets The Phantom of The Park!

Jan-Michael: You know how it was regarded, right? Everyone that loved Kiss, loved the movie. Nobody gave a shit about what it was, or was not, artistically. We — my script partner and I — got a press book from Hanna-Barbera about two months afterwards, with all the press clippings. There wasn't one positive review in North America! And yet, I have had people like yourself, who have said they loved and love it.

Ron: I think it was what it needed to be.

Jan-Michael: This is exciting for me ... is this the interview?

Ron: Well, it is kind of like a pre-interview.

Jan-Michael: Okay. In 1978, when we finished the first draft, we were told that Kiss wanted to see the script. And why not, right? So, copies of the draft went to their management company, which [which was run by a tough guy), Aucoin. Jesus, was he a tough son of a bitch. He had a whole room in his office filled with just Kiss merchandise. All the things they had licensed as of '78. It was amazing, the mountain of stuff. In fact, they gave me a Kiss radio, which I gave to my daughter. She met them all at Magic Mountain.

They fly us to New York after Kiss has had time to look at the script. Going in, we knew enough about the group, and we knew that none of these guys are actors. We gotta write like they are the Marx Brothers.

> **"At the time, we were a little annoyed — and that's putting it mildly."**

So, we get there, and here are the four guys. Peter Criss — nobody likes the drummer, ya know? So, I am waiting for the guys to say something — they don't like a scene, or maybe Abner. The first things we hear are from Criss, and Ace Frehley, and even Paul Stanley. They pulled out little papers, and they say *(adopts Ace-style voice)*: "It's a good script, but I only got 79 lines, and Gene got 322. What the fuck are you gonna do about that?"

Ron: They were comparing lines!

Jan-Michael: *Counting* lines! But actually, I thought Paul Stanley was a really sweet guy. And Ace Frehley was really a space cadet! But it was Gene I got to know the best. Because Gene has a fear of flying, and when we went out with them for a short time, he refused to let me sleep on their plane. He wanted to stay up and talk.

I tell ya, this is really cool for me; who the f*ck am I supposed to talk with about this? Once in a while my kid would tell me that she would run into someone who likes Kiss, and tell them I wrote the script.

I asked him (Gene) what brought him to this, and he said, "I was fat Jew-boy teaching school, making piss-all, and I'm looking around saying, 'I can do that.'" Gene is one of the smarter guys I have met in my lifetime. He told me so matter-of-factly how he put the band together, why he chose to do makeup.

> **"Gene is one of the smarter guys I have met in my lifetime."**

He said to me there were two reasons: one, he wanted to have something of a public life; he knew they were going to be so big. People *(in public)* might sense he was somebody. He was so tall, and always in platforms. I remember going to a restaurant with him in San Francisco — he teeters out of the limo, and everybody knew he was some kind of a rock star. The second reason he said was that with makeup, if anyone f*cks up, they're out of the group, no problem. He's telling me this in 1978, on the plane.

Ron: Who was the main guy you dealt with on the project?

Jan-Michael: Basically, Ron Roth ramrodded the project. Then there was Gordon Hessler. He was an English guy Hanna-Barbera hired because he did the *The Golden Voyage of Sinbad*. At the time, we were a little annoyed — and that's putting it mildly — that they didn't hire: a) a comedy director, and b) an American comedy director, who understood the nuances of the vernacular.

Ron: You wanted someone who could handle comedy?

Jan-Michael: Don (Buday) and I were not comedy writers, but it had a comedy strain. They really wanted an action movie, with some laughs. That is what they wanted. Something to showcase the group. The thing was, they tell you: "Use your imagination, boys. Come up with some really great shit that this group can do." You do it, and they say they can't afford to shoot it.

Ron: When I think about it, I sometimes can't believe that Hanna-Barbera was involved with this.

Jan-Michael: It's an interesting point. Why were they chosen to do the project? I think it was: 1. They had a lot of clout, and a production deal with NBC. 2. They *(HB)* wanted to break into doing projects like this, and 3. The network only knew numbers — they didn't know sh*t about the group. They probably saw the makeup, thought they were a bunch of clowns, and gave it to Hanna-Barbera!

Ron: It was a bit of superficial thing, then.

Jan-Michael: Absolutely.

Ron: On the band's side, the involvement of Hanna-Barbera was probably favorable because maybe it was felt that this could lead to a cartoon series.

Jan-Michael: Maybe.

Ron: The film was really supposed to be the first of many Kiss televisual ventures.

Jan-Michael: It was watched, there was no doubt about it. I don't remember the numbers. When it aired, I rented an Advent *(this was a big screen projection system)* and had a party. I remember my parents were in from Canada, and came. They lasted about 10 minutes watching it, and left the room!

Ron: Were your happy when you saw the finished production?

Jan-Michael: Was I happy? Um ... I was happy that they thing got made. But then, you want it made well. From that standpoint, particularly I wasn't happy with the direction. I didn't think that Hessler got those guys to do as best as they could do. Part of that, you have to put on the guys; it was a goof to them. Simmons took it seriously. I think if you look at the film, you could see that. Gene *tried*. They were basically four rock stars who showed up at the set and were fawned over. Nobody thought they were making anything great, to tell you the truth.

Ron: When you were at the set, did you pick up any feeling from them of, "uh-oh, what did we get ourselves into?"

Jan-Michael: Nah, I didn't feel that. It was like, "Sh*t, it's a take — oh well ... " They just did it. We were on the set all the time — the mansion, I was there at Magic Mountain, where they shot the robotic heads and stuff. I think in a tiny way, that movie was sort of ahead of everybody, with the mad scientists with the robotic heads *(laughing)*! I think without Zerbe, that movie would have floated away!

Ron: You had some prior writing experience before this.

Jan-Michael: We had a fair amount. We had written several movie scripts; one got sold, a couple of them got optioned, one got made. We didn't have a lot of television experience, which is one reason we wanted to do this. We figured, anything that Kiss is involved with, is going to lead to something.

Ron: How did you actually get this gig?

Jan-Michael: I believe we got the gig through somebody at our agency who knew Ron Roth. Someone called, and said they were looking for rock 'n' roll guys who are writers. We — Don and I — had written a script together, which was a black-oriented, R&B movie, that was sort of our version of *The Motown Story*. Instead of Barry Gordy, we had "Tripper Dupree," who was a street hustler. The long and short of it was, we write the thing, and it got optioned a half-dozen times. It never got made, it got us our agent. It was the calling card for most of the jobs we did get. Everybody thought we were black! If you were white, and could write black in Hollywood, that was big. That's how we got it *(Kiss Meets ...)* — it was through that script. Although, the Kiss thing wasn't really a music film.

> "It was watched, there was no doubt about it."

Ron: You hung out with Kiss for a while, right?

Jan-Michael: We went out with them on about four dates, in the Northwest. Portland, Seattle. Cheap Trick was the opener.

Ron: That's right! You saw *those* shows!

Jan-Michael: That's f*ckin' right! And let me tell you: that was a tough act to follow, for Kiss. It was a great idea, but putting on such a balls-out group like Cheap Trick to open, you gotta have a lot of balls yourself.

The main idea was to see them on stage, and get to know them a bit, off stage. It wasn't that easy, because Gene would just disappear into his hotel suite, and wouldn't be seen until showtime. I don't have to tell you what he was doing in there!

Ron: No, it's the stuff of legend!

Jan-Michael: I can tell you this: we were in their chartered plane, and we were flying south I think. We were sitting at a little card table. And Gene, like I told you, is afraid to fly. He's telling me his backstory, and at one point, he takes out this really nice bag, like a camera bag, a lovely leather one, and he dumps out all these Polaroids on the table. Each is of a different woman, with a number — this is right out of Cameron Crowe. Some were naked. Like a schmuck, I say, "Wow, that's from the whole tour?" He gives me this look and says, "Nah, that's just from today in Portland!"

Ron: Gene was realistically the best actor in Kiss.

Jan-Michael: Yes. He wasn't bad was a heavy.

Ron: Paul was okay?

Jan-Michael: What did Stanley do? He didn't try to act, did he?

Ron: Apparently, he was trying for a while, and he has done some cameos. And then, just last year, in Canada he did a run in *Phantom of The Opera*.

I think that Peter's acting was actually pretty good — his reactions were somewhat natural. There seems to be a slight emphasis on him in the script. A lot of references to him, things like "Melissa turns to Peter." I was wondering if you just picked a guy while writing, or thought that he would be good, and would become the breakout actor of the whole thing.

Jan-Michael: A Peter emphasis *(laughs)*? I don't think so. We hadn't met them when we wrote the first draft. It might have been because of the "Catman" name.

Ron: Speaking of which, there even seems to be some significant character development; it is mentioned how skilled he is in extreme karate, and so on. In the script, there are also things like a mention that there is a boy in Gene makeup, where in the movie, there is one in Peter makeup *(wow, the pro-Peter agenda going on here!)*.

Jan-Michael: Changes just happen, for production reasons. Although it may have had a decent budget for Kiss, it was still a TV movie of the week. I think we also wrote the script richer than they were able to shoot it.

Ron: How did you guys do financially from this?

Jan-Michael: I think we got as a pair $50,000 for it. That wasn't a bad piece of change for 1978. It was such a kick, the payday was a bonus. Getting hired to write it was amazing, and we just knew it was going to get on the air.

Ron: Did you ever hear any talk about a sequel, or developing a Kiss series?

Jan-Michael: Nah. I don't think they expected to do anything beyond that. Let's face it — the music was the bread and butter.

Ron: Bill Aucoin had some TV experience. Maybe that's why he was a ballbuster.

Jan-Michael: In his business, you had to be.

Ron: How old were you then?

Jan-Michael: We were in our late thirties. It didn't seem to matter, as we both had this music thing ... I'm a rock 'n' roller, all my life. I still am. That doesn't go away with age.

Ron: I wasn't sure if you would actually want to talk to anyone about *Kiss Meets The Phantom of The Park*.

Jan-Michael: Nah, we never had our ego in it that way. The point is, about the vision that

> "I was happy that they thing got made. But then, you want it made well."

we had, I don't think we blew up in our heads the vision of how good or bad the script was. I thought that we had written a decent, little script, that if it had been realized the way we had seen it in our heads, we felt that it really would have worked. But we also knew that going in, we couldn't expect too much from the group. And after they told us they were hiring this f*cking crazy Englishman as a director, I think in our heads, Don and I kind of bailed: "What's he going to do with the language? He's never directed comedy!"

Ron: When you are the writer, and you are on set, do you have any say?

Jan-Michael: Are you kidding? They don't want you there. If you are there, you are there as a guest. You don't give input.

Don Buday
Script Co-Writer
Interview conducted February 6, 2001

Like his writing partner Jan-Michael Sherman, Don has the contention that what was a strong script suffered while being filtered into the TV-movie format. He also has an interesting and unlikely opinion regarding the casting of a main character. Palpable is an overall fondness for his Kiss-related experience, and heck — as far as this author is concerned, he is *Kiss Meets ...* royalty! Let's get into the official *Conversations With Phantoms* interview with Don Buday!

Ron: The project happened smack-dab at the initial breaking point of the original band.

Don Buday: Yeah, I know. Peter was a weird guy. When we first worked with them, it was a cooperative situation, where they were all equal, but after a while, they just started treating them like sidemen (one can assume this is a reference to the great "Kiss divide," with Gene and Paul on side, and Peter and Ace on the other).

> "They started with the toughest stuff first, which I thought was a disadvantage."

Ron: How did you end up working on this project? I know you and Jan-Michael were working on a couple of screenplays prior to this.

Don: We had a history, and we were brought in by Hanna-Barbera. They wanted us to meet the band, because they felt they *(Hanna-Barbera)* were a little long in the tooth — they didn't think the band would relate to them. They wanted us to get to know these guys a little bit, which we did.

Ron: Do you remember the first time you met the band?

Don: I certainly do — we flew up to the Portland Coliseum. We went to their sound check, and Gene made us up in their makeup. We stayed and saw the show, and met up afterward. We were supposed to stay in Portland, and they were flying out. They said, "Why don't you come with us?" We were in our hotel rooms abut a half an hour, I guess! It was really weird; they were girls trying to scale up the side of the Hilton Hotel to meet these guys! We flew to San Francisco until about four in the morning. It was a really slow plane, a propjet. The same plane they used for their Can-Am Tour.

Ron: You mentioned the impression you had of Peter. What about the other guys?

Don: Well, Paul wasn't that outgoing. We didn't have much chemistry with Ace, but he was a nice enough guy. I do remember when they were filming, instead of pulling his punches, Peter threw a punch at an extra *(probably a stuntman)* and he didn't care if he hit the guy or not. I never sensed any animosity between them, but Gene was the guy who was the communicator. The whole thing was Gene's trip. He's Kiss, as far as I'm concerned.

Ron: Jan-Michael was mentioning working on script revisions with input from Kiss' manager, Bill Aucoin.

Don: I don't remember that. We did do another little trip. When they were getting ready to shoot, we flew back to New York, and spent a little time with Aucoin at his headquarters, and then we flew down to Virginia to look at an amusement park. We flew into Dulles, and looked at a place called Five Flags, or Seven Flags *(He was close — it was more likely the Six Flags park in Woodmore, Maryland. Coincidentally, in 1979, the independently owned Magic Mountain would become part of the Six Flags park chain).* We got along with Aucoin, and when we flew home, he gave us some Kiss paraphernalia.

> **"We wrote a lot of good stuff!"**

Ron: So, you scouted another park for this movie? *(It would have been really lame if Kiss made the movie on the East Coast — it would have lost its amazing late-'70's California flavor!).*

Don: Yeah. It was wintertime, and there was snow on the ground. It was hard to visualize. Terry Morse was with us. I don't know if we had written the script before that or after. It may have been the idea of letting the guys see what the locations would be like, so they could write against them. We of course ended up shooting out here, at Magic Mountain.

It would have been nice if we could of had the guys *(Kiss)* get some more experience under their belts before they filmed some of the more dramatic scenes. They started with the toughest stuff first, which I thought was a disadvantage. They got a lot better as they went along.

Ron: I think the script is pretty tight.

Don: What happened was, we wrote a script, and then there were a lot of changes. And a lot of [those] changes, we weren't happy about some of them. And then, Gordon Hessler was brought in to direct. He started probing into things, and some of the things he we wanted to do, we were like, "We did that already! We already wrote that!" So we gave him our first draft, and then he begins putting things back in! We felt kind of good about that.

They way they shot things was kind of wooden, I felt. Also, they shot a lot of this in daytime. They didn't shoot day-for-night, and it wasn't spooky enough. A lot of the scenes take place in the daytime, and I thought it lost a lot the sinisterism of it all. He *(Gordon)* was really nice; I just thought it could have been done a whole lot more creatively. And, Terry Morse was a prince of a guy.

"I don't feel Zerbe captured a madness."

Ron: Speaking of revisions, I have a copy of the script dated March 16, 1978, and it is also denoted as a final copy. But inside, it says it was revised on April 16! In it, there is a really cool log flume scene, where Kiss fights Indian *(as in "Native American")* robots.

Don: Yeah, I don't think that was shot. It was probably too expensive, or hard to do. We wrote a lot of good stuff! I was saying to Michael the other day that we really made a mistake in not having the guys autograph a script for us.

Ron: How about that intro scene, where it is explained how Kiss got their powers?

Don: I know … it was shot on a TV-movie of the week budget.

Ron: What else do you recall about the finished product?

Don: I thought one of the greatest scenes was Peter's (begins to sing "Beth") — that was a great song.

Hey, I gotta tell you, I came up with the gang members' names. There was a kid in my neighborhood in Detroit called "Slimey," so I loved the idea of calling one guy "Slime." I came up with "Dirty Dee." We thought for sure they would take that out, and they left it in! Who was the third one?

Ron: That would be "Chopper."

Don: Yeah, that wasn't a name I came up with; it may have been Michael's.

"It got a really good slot, but NBC never promoted it."

Ron: They are not officially referred to as such on screen, but in the script, that gang is called "The Lowriders."

Don: It was a Chicano thing; guys who had elongated shocks on their cars, they can make them go up and down.

Ron: What did you think of Anthony Zerbe?

Don: Uh, I thought he was good, but also thought he was miscast; we knew him from other work, but he didn't bring any of the madness we had in mind. It would have been nice to have somebody that was just a kook. Timothy Carey would have been *great*. I don't feel Zerbe captured a madness. With casting, you get who you can get, who's available *(Timothy Carey would have certainly given Zerbe a run for his money, if not topped his performance)*.

Again, we just thought if it had more night scenes … you can't make a horror film in daylight! You don't need much if you've got great lighting.

Ron: Well, the international version actually has *more* daylight scenes! As a script co-writer, you envisioned this story as being much darker in tone?

Don: If it were to be spooky, it should have been spooky. It was very campy. It was almost in the spirit of *Xena*, where everything is tongue-in-cheek. The only people that should have been funny in this were Kiss. You never wink at the audience. They just *happen* to be zany. They're the *Bowery Boys*, who happen to be up to their ass in spooky stuff.

Ron: So, how do you feel today about the movie and its reputation, where the word "camp" is almost always mentioned?

Don: I think its great.

Ron: How did you feel about the promotion of the movie leading up to broadcast?

Don: It got a really good slot, but NBC never promoted it. We thought it was going to be a perennial, since it came out close to Halloween. NBC dropped the ball; they didn't do anything with it. I watched NBC that Saturday morning it premiered, and they weren't promoting it. Kiss' crowd was a young crowd. Their demographic was like 9-14 or something. We figured NBC would run all kinds of promos to people that watch Saturday morning, to watch Saturday night. For whatever reason, to my knowledge, there were no ads. Movies of the week didn't get promoted until about 10 days before they get played. Here was an NBC show that was for that targeted audience, not promoted that day. That, I did not understand.

> "Gene loved it — he was a comic book fan."

Ron: You would think that especially given Hanna-Barbera's involvement, it would have happened.

Don: Exactly. I almost felt like there wasn't a champion [of the movie] at the network. I think what happened — and I could be dead wrong about this — I think the network hierarchy changed from the time we wrote the script to the time the show was finally played. I forget the chronology.

Ron: What did you do with your share of the *Kiss Meets ...* script writing loot?

Don: It wasn't that much money.

Ron: Michael gave me a figure of $50,000, for you guys to split.

Don: Hmmm. We were doing several things at the same time. I might have used it [the money] as a down payment on my house.

Ron: What was the writing process like?

Don: Michael and I used to write in both of our houses. We wrote it pretty quick. I can remember sitting in the front of his house, near the street. I was a pacer, and Michael liked to sit. I couldn't sit still. I remember walking around the driveway, I remember the brickwork ... we had a great time doing it.

Ron: How long did it take to write it?

Don: Not long, a couple of weeks. They don't give you too long in television. But we really liked it. I really feel that if it had been directed a little differently, had a little more of a budget, and promoted more by NBC, it would have been a lot better. Gene loved it — he was a comic book fan. They had their own Marvel comic.

Ron: The movie is sort of related to it. Although it was sadly un-filmed, the sequence of how Kiss got their powers, and the types of powers they have, is close to the comic story.

Don: They gave us a rough storyline beforehand that they wanted us to follow, and we went off from there.

Ron: So, that was really the only kind of writing bible they gave you?

Don: Yeah, they didn't give us the comic, though — I don't recall seeing that. There were some things they wanted included, like the talismans.

Ron: Did you go to the Magic Mountain concert?

Don: Yes, the press party. Michael and I were actually journalists, and covered the rock scene a lot. I wrote for the *Los Angeles Free Press*, as Michael did, and he did some writing for *Rolling Stone*, I did some for *Creem*. A lot of those people were there. They weren't surprised to see us there, but it was like, "Yeah, man — who are you here for?" I was like, "well, I *co-wrote this*." Most of these guys never got out of the "rock bag," if you will. They stayed in it; Michael and I went on to write television features.

Ron: When did you write for *Creem*?

Don: I'm not sure, but Lester Bangs was still there.

Ron: The vintage era! Did you watch any of the Kiss movie dailies?

Don: No — we didn't hang around that much. Nobody really wants the writers around *(laughs)*.

Terry Morse, Jr.
Producer

"We can just schmooze, and you can just ask me things." Just like that, Terry Morse, Jr. and I were off and running. It was a true producer's talk, too; although it had been forever since he had seen *Kiss Meets* ... his memories were sometimes as clear as if he were still on set.

Terry Morse, Jr.: I still have the cast and credit list. I haven't looked at it in a long time, as you can imagine. But I just looked at it, and see that we had to fire the cameraman. After the first week, Gordon Hessler came up to me, and said, "This guy is too slow. He is taking forever to light. I'll never do this. This is television, not a big feature." So, that Friday night, I had to fire him. His name is crossed out, and Bob Caramico *("Robert," credit wise, and he is also listed as "director of photography")* took over. A real slug-fast TV cameraman, that could get it done. I'm wondering what version you have seen.

Ron: Oh, I have seen both. In fact, I have repeatedly watched the theatrical cut in every available language dub!

Terry: They brought in a different editor [for that] — his name is Lou Lombardo, and he re-edited the picture and put some stuff back in it, and just moved stuff around. I don't know if it really is that much better or not, but they thought it might be better as a theatrical version. Basically, it's the same.

> **"The two powerhouses were Gene and Paul."**

Ron: Did you know the film was going to be released internationally and in theaters while making it?

Terry: No, but we always thought though, *why not?* We got a 35-millimeter negative, why not make it big screen? I don't know how it did.

Ron (in his mind): *I think it was a total blockbuster, everywhere!*

Terry: I'll tell you a little interesting thing: when we cast the picture, the part of "Sam" was an actor named Sam Cotten, and he was Joseph Cotten's son. When Joe Barbara saw the dailies, he said, "I want a surfer — a blond surfer." So, we had to let Sam go, and we hired Terry Lester. He became a soap opera star later on *(in the 1980s, as "Jack Abbot" on The Young and The Restless).*

(The senior Cotten was the super-legendary actor Joseph Cotten, who starred in Citizen Kane, so that means there is a —rather tenuous — connection of 'Kane to Kiss Meets The Phantom of The Park!)

Ron: He also has done some voice work.

Ron: How did you get involved in the Kiss project?

Terry: I was kind of the in-house line producer at Hanna-Barbera. We had done *The Gathering,* we had done *The Beasts Are Loose In The Streets,* and this was one of them we did. Deke (Heyward) was an executive working under Joe Barbera at the time. He was just around, shuffling papers. He was a good guy.

"It was a terrific concert, and we shot the hell out of it."

Ron: Do you recall Joe Barbera having cold feet about being involved on a Kiss project?

Terry: Yes — what you had said earlier about the tongue. Joe and Bill were cartoon people, and for kids, children. He was a little worried about being associated with it. In those days, Disney would never do anything like that, so that's what he was worried about: the Hanna-Barbera image, and these wild, hard rockers.

Ron: What was the first time you met the band members?

Terry: When we started casting — we brought them in for rehearsals, met them, talked to them. At that time, Gene was going with Cher. We had lunch with them, and kinda schmoozed. But they were kind of all off by themselves. They [each] had their own bodyguards, and they started to separate. The two powerhouses were Gene and Paul. Ace and Peter were really in the background, and they didn't like that, but that's just the way it was. Gene and Paul were the real personalities. I loved that song Peter did in the movie ("Beth"). I was never into their music; I like country and western.

It was different for me, working with them, but they were good guys. They each had to had the same Winnebago, their own stand-ins, and stuff like that. But they were fun to work with, and we had fun doing it.

Ron: About them being equal, their manager at the time, Bill Aucoin, told me that that they all sat down with the script and counted the number of lines they had. It was their only initial concern!

Terry: All actors are that way.

Ron: What I find interesting, and even funny, is that apart from Gene's rage scene, Kiss is only shown as a collective unit, all together, at all times.

Terry: They *are* always together!

Those great sets that Jim Hulsey built were in Culver City, which used to be part of MGM *(now Sony)*. That's where they shot *Gone With The Wind*. They have a couple of stages there, where the walls are made of glass — they used the sun for lighting. They're painted over now. Everything else was a practical location, including Kiss' "house." We shot inside, by the pool, and in front. [There was] that spooky set, where the girl screams ...

The scene with Gene bursting through the wall, with the silhouette? We beamed that on a stage wall. The concert, of course, was at Magic Mountain — you can see the roller coaster in some shots. I had four cameras going at the concert. It was a terrific concert, and we just shot the hell out of it! All of their songs — it was great.

Ron: There also were some lip-syncing performances filmed.

Terry: We also shot for coverage the next night; we couldn't get right in front of them *(at the concert)*. We shot parallel then.

Ron: A lot of that footage was not used.

Terry: There were a lot of trims. We had to come in at 92, or 96 minutes.

Ron: There was a whole scene in the original script that took place in New York, explaiing how Kiss got their powers. Was any of that filmed?

Terry: No. We also filmed a lot at the park, and for the day scenes, we actually owned the park. It was closed, for maintenance, and we went in with a couple of hundred extras. We did go in on a day it was open, and film some "wild" stuff, with a hand-held camera. When you see people on the rides, or going into the house of horrors, or coming out, that was all our extras there. Mary Kay, on the pyramid.

> *" ... we also dubbed Ace Frehley's voice, but it was so different ... "*

Ron: I was talking to Deke about the fact that there are several Universal monsters in the Chamber of Thrills scene, and he laughed, as if it was some kind of in-joke.

Terry: Oh, yeah! We just used them.

Ron: Well, it might be because of you as well as Deke that this movie is never released again *(laughs)*.

Terry: Why?

Ron: From what I can gather, Warner owns it now. And those are Universal properties.

Terry: Yes — we just used them. I don't think there would be a problem at this point. It has already been released.

Ron: Did you ever do any kind of screen tests with the band?

Terry: No. I mean, we had no choice *(laughs)*. Ya know, they were going to play the parts! In television, we usually don't screen the actors — we read with them, but we usually know who we want. Anthony Zerbe, by the way, is a wonderful actor.

Ron: What did you think of the female lead?

Terry: She was just another actress in those days; she's not acting anymore. In fact, she's a grandmother now!

Ron: Wow — that's more information right there than I have been able to find on her in two years!

Terry: I thought she was fine in the part, a pretty girl at the time. I thought all the cast was pretty good.

Ron: Carmine Caridi said he really had a good time.

Terry: Sure, everyone had a good time making the picture.

Ron: Except some of the guys in Kiss! And, speaking of Peter Criss, his voice was overdubbed by none other than Michael Bell.

Terry: Yes — and we also dubbed Ace Frehley's voice, but it was so different, that we just couldn't do it. It sounded crazy. We did that for enunciation; a lot of his *(Peter's)* stuff was unusable — you couldn't hear it, you couldn't understand it.

Ron: Would that Ace overdub still exist in some form, somewhere?

> "I hung out with all of them, but Gene was the most outgoing."

Terry: I don't think so. It was on tape, it was probably erased. Along with all the trims, it was probably discarded.

Ron: There wouldn't be any outtakes hanging around?

Terry: No — but maybe the master music tracks are around.

Ron: Do you have a copy of a rough cut or something?

Terry: No. I have the 3/4-inch [of the American TV edit]. I actually have both final versions, somewhere.

Ron: There perhaps was a cut of the whole movie with Peter's real voice, right?

Terry: There probably was, but that's all gone. We didn't put anything on VHS then, we worked off the film. We looked at dailies on the big screen. Have you ever seen the film on the big screen? There's a 35-millimeter print, somewhere.

Ron: I am still reeling from learning that Ace's voice had to be overdubbed.

Terry: It didn't have to be, we wanted to — but we went back to his own voice.

Ron: Did you ever hear any feedback from the band's management about any of the overdubbing?

Terry: No. There were sort of all over the world by that point; this was when the picture was done. In fact, I think we went back to New York to dub Ace, if I am not mistaken, where he lived at the time.

Ron: That is correct.

Terry: I don't remember; maybe he was out here. I think they both did their looping, and Peter's was so bad that we just replaced it, and then *(about Ace)* it sounded so crazy. He had such a distinctive voice. It wouldn't have been right.

Ron: Did you hang out with any Kiss guys on the set?

Terry: I hung out with all of them, but Gene was the most outgoing. At the time, as he was dating Cher, we had a chair for both she and Chastity on the set.

Ron: The concert shoot was a big deal, as a concert, and otherwise.

> "All you ever do is see them screaming on stage, and here they are, doing dialogue, talking about things."

Terry: Yeah. There were a lot of news people out there, a lot of executives from Taft Broadcasting. I don't know if Joe and Bill Barbera were, I'm not sure. It was a wild night. We shot everything, and the next day, we got up on the stage, and shot each guy three or four times, to get good, clean close-ups. We couldn't do that at the show, with long lenses that would go out of focus. We did it to make the guys look good *(and there are some truly awesome shots in those close-ups)*.

Ron: What did you think about the project at the time?

Terry: It was a hoot! It was fun.

Ron: What did you think of the script?

Terry: The script was *okay*; it was not a great piece. I don't think the writers did anything after that. Neither of them were great writers, but it was what it was: a campy —

Ron: — but was it intentionally campy, though?

Terry: No.

Ron: What do you think brought that out? Kiss not being able to act, the direction?

Terry: No, it was just Kiss, being in a movie. Them, acting. All you ever do is see them screaming on stage, and here they are, doing dialogue, talking about things *(laughs)*. That was what I considered campy.

Ron: Did you see the new Kiss movie?

Terry: I think I saw that, but they *(Kiss)* didn't do acting.

Ron: Right — they are like a "Wizard of Oz" entity in it. What is interesting is that in the *Kiss Meets ...* script there is a scene where Peter throws a drumstick to an elated fan, and there is a scene like that in *Detroit Rock City.*

Terry: I remember that! Those guys should get together and do another movie. I think there would be a lot of interest in it.

Ron: I think Gene is trying to do a cartoon series. On a related note, I spoke to Lou Scheimer *(of Filmation animation studio)* and apparently Kiss was almost going to go with a cartoon series, in lieu of a live-action project. Then, the Hanna-Barbera thing came along, with Deke Heyward pushing for live action. I'm also thinking that maybe Kiss management figured that an animation deal would have been relatively easy to get.

Terry: Yes.

Ron: The scoring is very campy. There will be an action scene, with goofy music underneath it! Of course, the international cut replaced most of that with Kiss tunes, from their solo albums, which worked for the most part.

Terry: Hoyt *(Curtain, the movie's music composer)* was not ... he just did music for Hanna-Barbera cartoons! He was not a big talent. Hanna-Barbera insisted we use him; he was an in-house composer.

Ron: Do you recall how much it cost to have this movie made?

Terry: I haven't the slightest idea. But usually, we did these for two, two-and-a-half million.

Ron: When I had spoken to co-scriptwriter Don Buday, he felt that the film could have been darker if they shot day-for-night.

Terry: Well, day-for-night looks terrible! What do writers know about that? You shoot during the day, and you can see the sky, mountains in the distance, you don't see that at night. You only see what you light, at night. So, day-for-night wouldn't have worked.

PHANTOM FINDINGS
Gene Wasn't The Only One To Break A Wall

In film and television, "breaking the fourth wall" refers to characters stepping out of scenes and directly addressing the audience. It can happen anywhere in a story, and happens fast, as to not derail things. Essentially, they are cool little Easter eggs. The technique has also evolved to sometimes become a major part of a TV show or film. An actor may break the wall often, but stay in character, to share thoughts, motivations, and the like. It can sometimes be an overly cutesy, and cop-out way of storytelling, but it is almost always fun.

The makers of *Kiss Meets The Phantom of The Park* (our "Phantom Fathers") undoubtedly had absolutely none of this in mind when filming — though about a half hour into the movie you could imagine Calvin Richards addressing the camera and saying, "this Abner is becoming a real pain in the *ss!" (Of course, that would have to had appeared in the movie-house edition.)

With lots of filming happening inside Magic Mountain (controlled sets and "wild" shots), and then at the Kiss performance in its parking lot, there were bound to be some lens lookers (Excusably, the concert scenes are loaded with them, to cool effect). Most are less than one second long or thereabout, and not distracting. Some are worthy of examination, for various reasons.

Take a *look* at the ones below from the *Attack of The Phantoms* edit.

1) At 4:15 during the makeup contest scene, a child in Gene makeup looks at the camera, complete with a blank expression that suggests he rather be *anywhere* else. The overall shot of the group of Kiss kids is a good one, which is probably why it was kept in spite of this boy's non-adherence to general on-camera rules.

2) This one is interesting, because it involves a couple of principals. It is a tough one to see, but at 4:46 Sam and Melissa are looking either right at a camera, or perhaps Gordon Hessler, right next to one, waiting for a cue to start walking down the steps of The Revolution ride. Check out the expressions of total happiness they are wearing — they were not seen again anywhere in either edition of the movie.

By the way, after getting the green light to move, they make it about all of 10 feet before being trapped from the main walkway (and in the shot's background) by the marching band (in the foreground). *This* is where the Phantom Fathers decided (and it is in both versions) to have Sam set up the story a little bit, with a couple of voiceover lines (exclusive to each edit, and odd) that were unspoken on camera! When Sam bails from the scene, he has to deftly cut through the sea of moving musicians.

By the way, despite its having like a million students in it, the Canyon High School marching band actually did a great job of not looking at the camera (though some marchers' full-on smiling sometimes threatened to suspend the suspension of disbelief).

By the way more, this scene is also noteworthy for while Sam begins to play *Frogger*, you can see the crummy Lowriders exiting a building, and making their entrance into the movie. It is well done, and the closest they would get to being in a scene with Sam or Melissa. Except, of course, later on in Abner's lab, after being abducted and losing control of their minds.

3) The guy in Kiss makeup working as part of the Kiss merchandise stand at 13:09 is something else. He was obviously an extra, and should have known better. Regardless, he just really goes for it. This guy is kind of an oddball — earlier, he is seen using a rather aggressive attention-getting tactic of tapping a guy on his arm who is checking out a Kiss radio. This dude must have been a bootleg concert shirt salesman in real life.

4) At 59:39 (*why* is this amazing scene seen so late in the movie?) Space Ace – that's right, a Kiss member — looks at the camera. It happens at the Colossus roller coaster, after

Kiss walks into the scene, Paul drags his right leg a few times, does his disco walk/strut, while still dragging his leg, and Peter/Michael Bell says, "apes is more like it." Blink and you'll miss it, but it is there.

Louis M. "Deke" Heyward
Executive in Charge of Production
Interview conducted February 2002

Deke is a legend in terms of creating kitschy Hollywood coolness, and the entire interview experience with him was as entertaining and fun as his work. After exchanging emails, we arranged to speak in person at his home, during the first of my pair of 2002 California sojourns done for this project.

Pre-interview notes: "Killer Kenny" was with me on this trip, a six-feet four knock-around guy of the highest order, and fountain of information about seemingly all things. After demanding I drive him to the Hollywood Forever cemetery upon our West Coast arrival — watching him walk around obsessively looking for Carl "Alfalfa" Switzer's grave was worth it — he would prove his worth in this meeting, as his extensive celluloid knowledge came in handy.

The interview was scheduled on the final day of our Cali stay. After checking out of our hotel — where in the lobby Kenny kept calling me "boss" in front of confused onlookers and staff — we jumped into our rental car and headed north up the Pacific Coast Highway. We made a right turn somewhere after Zuma Beach. and then started heading up a mountain in a steep, spiral fashion, going around and around until there were no more houses. Soon, there was no more street, but there was a gate. Kenny jumped out and rang a buzzer.

Voice Through Buzzer Speaker: Who's there?

Killer Kenny: Uh, I'm Kenny, and I have Ron Albanese with me. We are scheduled to see Mr. Heyward.

Speaker Voice: Let me open the gate — and then you can just drive up to the house.

We passed through the gate, and twisted and turned a bit more until we were right at the front door of the residence. Deke's wife warmly greeted us, ushering us into the living room. She put out some wine, which we sipped while looking through floor-to-ceiling windows at the both the ocean (in front of us) and trees (behind us).

Suddenly, we heard a voice: "she likes that view, I like this one." It was Deke (*and he preferred the ocean view*).

We all sat down, I turned on my cassette recorder, and *Kiss Meets The Phantom of The Park* class was in session.

Deke: Have you met Bill Aucoin?

Ron: Yes, I have met him a couple of times, and have interviewed him for this book.

Deke: My recollection of him is that he was a damn nice guy. Very outgoing, very much for the group, and trying to negotiate the best deal he could for them, and for himself. Somehow — I can't tell you exactly how — my son Andy was responsible for our introduction. He was at his own company by that point — at DIC Entertainment. No, wait ... .

Ron: Maybe he was doing something at Filmation?

Deke: Yes. He was at Filmation, working with Lou Scheimer, and [while the film project was being pursued] he was trying to get the rights to do Kiss, animated, from Bill Aucoin. And naturally, [we as] father and son were like, "uh-huh, yeah!" (*as in competing*): "you're younger than me? I'm older than you are. You may be stronger, but ... " It was all good-natured. Somehow or another, I seduced Aucoin — with Aucoin's help, very much with his help — into doing the picture.

> **On Bill Aucoin:**
> **"My recollection of him was that he was a damn nice guy."**

"The picture" — what *was* the picture? That was a euphemism. There was no picture. Jan-Michael Sherman, and Don Buday — a Hungarian guy, and a Polish guy — were sweethearts, they were wonderful. I told them what we had

70   *Conversations with Phantoms*

rattling around: automated figures, of a band, kind of left over from the days of Dr. Phibes. Have you ever seen that?

Kenny (excitedly): Yes! ("Dr. Phibes" refers to a pair of early-1970's cult classic films that Deke produced, starring Vincent Price: The Abominable Dr. Phibes, and Dr. Phibes Rises Again.)

Deke: Well, we had that automated thing, and we used that as a jumping point for making this. Again, you should know who the players were: there was Bill Hanna. Bill was the nicest, nicest man in the world. If you were to think of someone very talented to play Pink Rabbit ... he looks like Pink Rabbit. He smiles at you, and he looks like a schoolteacher, but he knows his business. He's got a got a partner, a rock 'em, sock 'em ... it's good cop, bad cop: Joe Barbera. Joe is the guy who was like, "let's sell this!" and it was like, "but Joe, we don't have it!" and he was like, "let's sell it, anyway!" It's good that way. And there was always this continuing schism, between Joe and Bill, [to the point] that Joe was not permitted to go to Bill's funeral.

> "It would be nice to turn them into people who were loveable, and could become animated people."

Ron: It got that bad?

Deke: Yes, they were looking for someone to be between them. I had my background of having made movies all over Europe, and for Universal. Obviously, nobody is going to stand up to Joe Barbera and Bill Hanna in animation. But when you come to motion picture operation, yes, I could stand up to them. So, he *(Bill)* brought me in there. I was made "executive in charge of production." My job was to bring him live productions of the type that would be in line with the name Hanna-Barbera. And, to try to get ratings — because they were in the process of trying to divest themselves of investors and business connections they had in the Midwest somewhere. They wanted to win awards, they wanted to make a run of it themselves. My background in AIP *(American International Pictures)* seemed to indicate that I was the guy for them. The first picture I did for them was *The Gathering*, with Ed Asner and Maureen Stapleton. We won "Best Production of The Year" at the Emmys, and that too got a theatrical release, which surprised me, because we weren't trying for theatrical releases. We got great reviews, and awards, from the Humanities award and so on.

Yes, we wanted to do something that the kids could relate to — instead of having thieves as people, of which kids would be afraid — and they *were* afraid of them during this period — it would nice to turn them into people who were lovable, and could become animated people. And, it would have happened, except that I allowed Joe Barbera to see the dailies on this thing. Now, he did not know who Kiss was, or what Kiss was.

Ron: That's surprising!

Deke: Well, Joe was so far away from kids. In contrast to my son! Uh, I'd invite Joe to see the dailies — and he says, "You got this sick guy, and I don't know — shouldn't we wait until he gets better?"

(Whispering, as if discretely talking to Joe on the set, about Gene Simmons' sticking out of his tongue) "That's his whole act, Joe! Draw your own inferences!"

> **"It really did not appear they could walk too good with those shoes."**

"You mean, this is what he does? Like with *girls*? We can't have it!" I said, "I can't put his tongue back in his mouth, Joe. This is his act, this is what he does." So, he says he's not going to come down [to the set], and he didn't. He didn't see one day of shooting.

Ron: Really? Not one day?

Deke: No. But he betrayed some total goofiness. There are about six scenes, where Gene does the tongue bit. And [later], I come into Joe's office, and he's got a mobile unit, and a couple of editors there, and he was trying to get the tongue back into the mouth!

Ron: Was he trying to cut scenes?

Deke: No. He just wanted the tongue back in the mouth — it scared him! He thought it was dirty!

Let's go back: I had introduced him to Gordon Hessler. Gordon was at Universal when I was at Universal. I was head of live action. Gordon was in a much better situation than I was — he was the protégé for Alfred Hitchcock. He was Hitchcock's darling. And, to a guy who was doing stand-up comics, which was what I was doing at Universal ... [I was impressed]. I too was doing work with Hitchcock, so I got to be friendly with Gordon. And time passes by, we all disappear. I become head of AIP — I am in charge of all the foreign [productions]. I wanted somebody to work with, who I had confidence in. You had French directors, who will screw you, English directors, who mostly party another way. I run into Gordon Hessler in England: "Gordon, I need you. I want you, I love you." And Gordon did six pictures for me in a row, in England. He was like my good-luck coin. My Hollywood people were bigger, but maybe not for the types of pictures I was doing; down and dirty, *get in fast, get out fast*. I latched onto the guy who had done *The Avengers*, Bob (Robert) Fuest. And, Gordon lost a job with me — because I had Bob Fuest — to do *Wuthering Heights*. However, once I had come back to the United States, I didn't have Bob Fuest any longer — "Gordon, where are you?" I think this *(Kiss Meets ...)* is the first thing he did for me here. And then, we suffered in Canada for about five months, shooting with a Polish guy — like an Anthony Quinn type. Anyway, I started with Gordon again, and we did pictures.

Okay, so you got a little before, you got a little after, here's the middle. Everybody was nervous; we didn't know what the hell we were gonna do with these guys. First of all, it really did not appear as though they could walk too good with those shoes *(laughs)*. They appeared to be off-center, and concessions had to be constantly made. Buddy Joe Hooker — a nice guy — he helped them on virtually everything they had to do. I don't know what they have told you about their participation, for a large part of the violent scenes, the body movement scenes, the heights scenes, they were out of it. They couldn't handle it. And, it is kind of obvious.

Ron: The movie was universally panned —

Deke: — but it got ratings.

Ron: The scriptwriters indicated that they thought NBC sort off dropped the ball promotion and hype wise.

Deke: They were scared. They didn't know what they had, they didn't know what these guys were. [To them] they were dangerous and crazy people.

Ron: I understand that Ron Roth was instrumental in getting NBC to understand the band and project.

Deke: That's true. He was a friend of Gordon's. Also, Sal Fischer was an agent for Hanna-Barbera, and was tight, tight with NBC. He moved down to our offices, but then worked on movies of the week.

The Gathering had begun its genesis in my own family. I'm ex-Air Force, and my son stayed out of the Army — which was a big hurt to me — during the days of the Vietnam War. And the fights we had were "old Army vs. a bad war." That's what *The Gathering* was about. The father couldn't get in his head why his son didn't want to go fight in the Army. That was me. We pitched 28 shows to NBC that year; we sold 24 shows. The 24 shows were sold in one afternoon, starting off with *The Gathering* — where I knew what I was talking about — going into Kiss, where I had vague ideas, into a thing called *The Beasts Are Loose*, which is the story of a cougar who wanders into an operating room in Palm Springs, while a hard operation was going on. I was just spinning. The funny thing was the NBC guy, he went back to, "how dirty is this?" [about Kiss]. So, we arranged that if he bought the show movie, it *(Gene's sticking out of his tongue)* wouldn't happen more than four times.

> **On Joe Barbera:**
> **"He was scared sh*tless."**

Ron: He too, was hung up on Gene's tongue.

Deke: Yes. We arranged that if he bought it, it wouldn't happen more than four times in the course of an hour!

Ron: Wow.

Deke: Well, this is all stupid things.

Ron: Was the *Legends of The Superheroes* roast in this package?

Deke: Yes.

Kenny: Excellent!

Deke: It had through-the-sky ratings. It was written by a guy named Mike Marmer. When I was working on the Ernie Kovacs show, he was my assistant. I had reached the point, where I didn't want to write, and Mike may have done a jazzing up of gags on this *(Kiss Meets ...).*

Ron: He polished it up?

Deke: Yes — he may have. I'm all over the lot now! Am I confusing you?

Kenny: No — I love Ernie Kovacs.

Deke: He was so good.

Ron: Here's a Kiss script I have with me — this a first draft ...

Deke: How did you get this?

Ron *(getting wordy)*: Since I announced doing this project, people from all over the world have been sending me things. I have another script, too, dated April 16th of '78, which has some different scenes. Regarding Filmation, do you know if any concept art was ever drawn up, to present to the band or something?

Deke: They must have done, I believe they had done, I would not swear that they had done, a pencil test. Limited animation, but done only in pencil.

Ron: That would be amazing to finally learn — I'm trying to detail all of Kiss' superhero appearances, and the Filmation thing ... wow.

Deke: Yes. It was a different time, then. We weren't making much money, but we were getting good seats in restaurants.

Ron: Do you remember the first time you met Kiss?

Deke: Yeah. Bill Aucoin brought them over to Hanna-Barbera, in the Valley, and they were trying to shock us. Either somewhere there, or in a van before they got there, they got into makeup and costumes before they came into my office. I ran into Joe Barbera's office laughing — and Joe Barbera got scared! Joe had a red light; if it came on, no one could go in [his office]. The buzzers were locked. I just remember these four idiots clopping through our back lot on their high-heeled shoes, and Gene doing *(does Gene-style faces and tongue wagging)* ... and Joe, looking out his window, and suddenly, the red light goes on, and there ain't nobody going in *(laughs)*!

> "Gordon was the best budget director in the world."

Ron: He didn't want to see them?

Deke: He was scared sh*tless. You see, some people are scared of clowns, spiders ... .

Ron: Right! The mind just locks in on some over-the-top fear.

Deke: Joe was really scared, but he should have known better. When we went to do our pictures in New York, we'd do the same thing *(have HB characters show up)*.

Ron: Kiss were just trying to impress.

Deke: Yes. Tell me more about their manager, Bill Aucoin; my memory of him is not full, I remember I liked him a lot.

Ron: Bill Aucoin was a very likable person, and something of a mastermind. Prior to Kiss, he had some television producing experience, on a show called *Flipside*, which spotlighted music artists.

Deke: Yes.

Ron: His show was like a step past *Shindig*.

Deke: How do you know about *Shindig*?

Ron: It was a required stop for so many music artists — and I'm stuck in the past!

Deke: I did one of those, and I worked with Dick Clark, who is my best friend, and the nicest human being in the whole world. We did the first integrated show in Atlanta, and the KKK was after us — they threatened to burn us down. We had to bring in guards from another state. I asked him if he really wanted to do it, and he wanted to do it.

Ron: Who *haven't* you worked with?

Deke: If you live long enough, you end up doing it all — all you gotta do is stay alive!

Ron: Going back to those first encounters with Kiss, did you put them through screen tests?

Deke: No. Absolutely not. Gordon is an Englishman, and doesn't like noises. So, when these guys (Kiss) came up, with those loud noises, [it was] severe headaches. Anyway, Gordon got along with them, because he has the slightest bit of an English accent, and he would be very hesitant: "Could you give me a quarter of an inch more ... would that be possible?" It was the vaguest intensity. A dear, sweet, good man.

Ron: I heard two main things from the writers about him.

Deke: Good or bad?

Ron: Both. On the plus side, they said he went through great pains to give Kiss crash-course acting lessons on the spot.

Deke: This is true.

Ron: Because, they were really wooden.

Deke: This is true.

Ron: On the minus side — and keeping in mind these are writers, and when you see your work fleshed out in different medium, it can be jarring — they thought that the film could have been more convincingly evil if he shot day-for-night. That's actually what Don Buday said.

Deke: That was not Don Buday's decision, that was not Gordon's decision; that was *my* decision. And, everything boils down to equation of costs: what you're getting for the thing, and how much you're going to sell it for.

Ron: Kiss' people put out that *Kiss Meets* ... was the most expensive TV film made to that point, with a budget of two million dollars. I am thinking the budget was actually a little lower.

Deke: Uh, we brought that bugger in for $750,000. But, nobody in the world could have done that, except Gordon Hessler. Gordon was the best budget director in the world.

Ron: There is a significant amount of blue screen work in the film, which may have eaten up a big piece of the budget?

Deke: No, because at the time, you were getting things for free: "Try it, see how it works ... ."

I want to show you something. So, Buddy Joe Hooker says to me, "All right, we got these cockamamie, cybernetic ... " whatever they were. He then said, "You get into a costume, you get up there *(on the roller coaster framework)*, and when you come down, I'll give you this belt *(reveals a belt with a Stuntmen's Association member belt buckle on it)*." I couldn't find a harness that fit me — most of the guys were small. I climbed up, anyway. And I froze. And he had to send the monkeys after me. When I came down, he said, "You get this belt, anyway!"

(About the costume heads) Those things looked like cats. Pussycats. I started cutting off the whiskers with scissors; "I know enough about ornithology — or whatever it is *(we all laugh)* to know apes don't have whiskers. The costume manager was in hysterics: "Every one, you cut off, it costs you fifty bucks."

(Switches gears) Anthony Zerbe ... I sort of remember something petty happening, like we were impinging on his lunch hour. Joe Barbera, he just didn't understand what he was getting into. [He was just like] "Who wears shoes like that?"

Ron: What made *you* accept Kiss right away?

Deke: My background with Dick Clark.

Ron: Did you actually consult with him prior to taking on this project?

Deke: I may have. I still see Dick once a week. My son is the administrator of his estate.

Ron: So, you saw Kiss' potential, in terms of reaching a kids' audience? What about Hanna-Barbera turning Kiss into a cartoon?

Deke: Of course. That's what they bought them for, *we* bought them for. Oh, yeah. There was no question. I do think they could have been animated. Now, how that fell apart, I can't tell you. I do think it was Joe Barbera's total discomfort with them. You know, even in those days, stars — and they were stars — liked to have a number-one guy come in (I was number two) and say: "How are you? Everything all right? Can I get you anything?" Joe was afraid of those people.

Ron: Was there ever talk of doing another live-action feature with them?

Deke: No. Television moved on, we moved on. When I can do superheroes, I don't have to build ... if you remember, the only one who was really there was Adam West.

Ron: The *Shazam!* guy was there —

Kenny: — but he was a more of a Saturday morning thing —

Deke: — he was there because of Lou Scheimer.

Ron: There was Frank Gorshin, but yeah, many of the other people were like beginners.

Deke: Yeah, and the thing to remember is that these were primetime shows, and they knocked the hell out of everything else.

Ron: Did you go to any of the premieres for *Kiss Meets ...* or the party at Magic Mountain?

Deke: No. I didn't know about them (the premieres). I was called for tickets for the party; a newspaper writer called me for them, for all his children. I also got requests for albums!

Ron: There was reportedly some extra security at Magic Mountain, for the concert.

Deke: We just spread the word: "Anyone that wants to come can come," and let me tell you, it was scary.

Ron: The park was not totally open during filming right?

Deke: No. And it *(the Colossus roller coaster)* was not yet completed. We also had the run of the park.

PHANTOM FINDINGS
How Kiss Went Camping, Thanks To Abner's Uncle

Throughout this author's *Kiss Meets ...* research and interviews, it is abundantly clear that there is a common idea among its viewers (besides the general assessment of Peter Criss) that the movie's campy vibe stemmed from things like the band's and others' acting, the story, (non-Kiss) costuming, scoring, *and* the fact that it mostly takes place in an amusement park. All of that may be true (and wow, that's a lot) but there is also another, overlooked source: Deke Heyward.

A review of his body of work reveals a plethora of projects rife with campy comedy. For example: the gloriously tacky *Dr. Goldfoot and The Girl Bombs* (a 1966 sequel to 1965's awesome *Dr. Goldfoot and The Bikini Machine*) is practically nothing but camp (Franco and Ciccio were even part of the cast — look them up). It is also particularly notable in relation to *Kiss Meets The Phantom of The Park*, as it too features a mad scientist ("Dr. Goldfoot," played by Vincent Price), hell-bent on destruction. What's more, he was trying to do it with an army of self-designed automatons (though they are beautiful women, and not various people like Sam). Dr. Goldfoot can most definitely by considered a spiritual antecedent to Abner Deveraux, if not his wacky uncle, which would blend the *Goldfoot* and *Kiss Meets ...* universes. Deke was both a producer *and* writer on this one.

Then, there are other things Deke did, like *The Ghost in The Invisible Bikini* (serving as a writer) and *Pajama Party*, which he actually solely wrote. Let that sink in: the "Executive In Charge of Production" for *Kiss Meets The Phantom of The Park* is the same person who wrote the beach movie style comedy and kitschy classic, *Pajama Party*.

Given the leanings of his oeuvre — a good portion of which involved Gordon Hessler, by the way — it's a safe bet that his presence on the set brought out some Kiss camp. It is almost surprising that the finished product was not campier — and didn't have a cameo by Frankie Avalon.

Gordon Hessler
Director
Interview conducted August 2002

I first made contact with Mr. Hessler via email, and would eventually have the privilege of interviewing him in person at his home in Hollywood Hills.

Immediately upon my arrival, the *Kiss Meets ...* director proved to be a personification of the term "English gentleman." He brought me into a main living room area that was both classic and classy. It was also understated; barring a retrctable movie screen hanging from the ceiling, the space offered no other visible hint of the man's profession.

"Look at this," he said, opening doors to a balcony that overlooked the greater Los Angeles area. As I took in the view, Gordon retreated to his kitchen, and returned with some tea and a strawberry-covered cake. We settled in, dug in, and began talking.

Ron: How did you get this job?

Gordon Hessler: Deke [Heyward, Executive in Charge of Production] called me, and said, "I have a project I would like you to do." Since I knew Deke — I had made several pictures with him through AIP *(American International Pictures)* — I came in, he gave me the script, and we were off and running.

Ron: You just kind of jumped in?

Gordon: Back then, I *had* to take it. I was taking everything. I don't know if Deke originally had somebody else in mind. If so, that director may not have been able to do it. All I know is that I received a telephone call. I didn't know any of the group's history. These kinds pictures are very difficult to make, because basically there are so many special effects involved, and you don't have any time or money. Unless, you plan them very thoroughly, like a war, none of the elements come together. And then, you have a company *(Hanna-Barbera)* that is unfamiliar with special effects. You know, you could not convince the production people here in Hollywood to use the tools that were available, such as more blue screen. I took them to a studio that could do the work moderately cheap. But it was complicated to them, so we went for the most reliable and cheapest way, which was mostly black screen. It was literally black velvet; you put the actors in front of it, and put the opticals in during post-production, as opposed to doing a great deal of the work while you are shooting, which makes it much simpler. It actually complicated the whole process. On reflection, the special effects were acceptable, but mediocre.

> "There were a number of elements interfering with each other."

Ron: Are you saying blue screen wasn't used at all?

Gordon: No, none. Like where Kiss walked over the fountain — that was just black steps and velvet. They *(Hanna-Barbera)* were so terrified! Nobody there knew how to do a picture like this in three, four weeks. The special effects were done by two guys in a laboratory!

(Blue screen was used, as evidenced in photos and referenced in the official Kiss Meets The Phantom of The Park magazine, published in 1978. So, while Gordon may seem wrong, he still may be right; blue screen use seems to have been relegated solely to the opening sequence. The director may have been making a distinction between filming the movie's scenes, and the beginning credits, which actually contain both blue and black screen use!)

Ron: On the positive side, the film's opening sequence is effective in establishing the main setting, introducing Kiss, and is exciting.

Gordon: I vaguely remember shooting it. We had them [Kiss] for the whole day in the studio.

Ron: In Culver City, where they shot *Gone With The Wind*?

Gordon: Yes — I was walking around in awe! Terry Morse was responsible for getting the whole team together there.

Ron: Many people have said that you were basically giving the members of the band acting lessons on the set.

Gordon: Yes, they were awkward, in funny way. They were shy of the whole project, and yet they were anxious to do the best they can. When you're a singer, you're on the top of the world, on big stages in front of 10,000 people. When you're an actor, and you have to have a camp style, it's difficult, even for somebody who is a trained theater artist.

Ron: Are you saying that you thought the project was purposely camp?

Gordon: No. But you couldn't take the script seriously. It was written by two young fellows, who were very talented. But you couldn't do the effects; there was no physical way of doing the effects that they had in the original script. I wouldn't know *how* to do it. Certainly not in three weeks. It would have been a total lack of responsibility [to try to do them]. All of these things required infinite preparation. They would have been financially exhausted. So you compromise it all the way down the line.

Ron: There you were, with a far-reaching script. Then, you have the stars themselves, who are making their first movie ever. And, you have about three-and-a-half weeks to deliver this thing.

Gordon: Yes. *That* is the problem I was tackled with, and you just try to work your way through, one day at a time. A director in movies of the week has to bring pictures in on time — one day late, they wouldn't like you. One week late, they would probably think about replacing you.

Ron: I have heard that some time lost was due to helping Kiss members act better.

Gordon: Time was lost. And I didn't have much to do with the casting. It was already cast, which is most unusual for a director, but *Kiss* was the cast! The girl, I had never seen, never worked with her. Then again, you don't interview Anthony Zerbe, because he was quite well known at the time. You accepted the name. When we did a day or two of shooting, whoever they used as the male lead, they didn't like. Deke Heyward came down and said that they didn't like the rushes, that he couldn't carry the part, and they are replacing him.

Ron: That was Sam Cotton as "Sam" — was there much footage shot with him?

Gordon: Oh, yeah. I remember it was about two days [of] shooting. I didn't think he was that bad, actually. But I didn't see it on a screen.

Ron: You weren't seeing any footage while working?

Gordon: No. We were at Magic Mountain, there at night, too — I was just shooting away. The first day I met Kiss, I asked if I could have a rehearsal. Most major stars don't want to do it. But Kiss agreed to do it, and on a Sunday, the day before we started shooting. They came in, and we spent the whole day going through the script. Reading it out loud. It was quite an experience, because normally it's a thing that actors do; they also discuss the role, the parts. In this case, they arrived with their bodyguards and personal servants! I offered them something to eat, meaning coffee and a donut, something like that. And it was like, "oh, yes — I'll have eggs Benedict!" They were out there. I didn't even know where to get that, but sure enough, suddenly it appeared. Anything they wanted. They were a bit shy, and rather overwhelmed. They were enormously popular people in their world; they could dictate anything they wanted, and it would be produced instantly.

Gene Simmons was the most intelligent of the group — he was a schoolteacher — and he liked horror pictures. He was interested, fascinated, in the business of acting and so on, and helped me a great deal. If I had a problem, I could talk to him. They were all nice, but I didn't get to know the others as much as I did Gene. He seemed to be the leader, and Paul Stanley seemed to be *kind* of a leader. The others were much farther in the background. Gene was also much more communicative than the others. I remember the absolutely crazy party he had for Cher on Sunset. He had this tremendous party, planes flying overhead. He had a tank with dwarves come down Sunset Boulevard. She was very diminutive, silent. He was very keen on this girl.

Ron: I wanted to ask about filming outside. On May 19, Kiss performed their concert show at Magic Mountain.

Gordon: Funny enough, that concert was terribly easy to shoot. It was an event that was happening, that you really have no control over. I just set up seven cameras. I was wondering how we would get people, and Aucoin said it was no problem. I thought maybe three, four thousand people, and I think maybe ten thousand were actually there. The only thing I had to do as a director was, when the bad Kiss came out, was talk to the audience: "Okay, this is what is happening. I want you to react to this."

Ron: Do any particular scenes stand out for you?

> "These were really stock characters; they weren't very good."

Gordon: I loved the sequences where we had mime people. They were wonderful, I thought. It came to life. If I were doing a feature film, I would have quickly had the writers write something more for the mimes, as part of the action and villainy. Fascinating things, we could have done. In television, you have no time to rewrite.

Ron: I thought the "Gene rage scene" was cool. It is something of an homage to a number of horror movies.

Gordon: I remember the scene. It was very easy to get the cameraman to shoot the shadow *(laughs)*. It was routine picture making.

Ron: Do you recall there being any issues regarding any members of the group's speaking voices? One was eventually replaced.

Gordon: It's not that uncommon in the business. Actors don't like to do looping, as it is an imitation process. The actor is furious when he has to do it.

Ron: Spontaneity can be lost?

Gordon: Yes, they have to remember exactly how they did it.

Ron: There are a significant number of scenes in the earlier versions of the scripts that were not filmed, including a backstory about how Kiss got their powers, taking place in New York City.

Gordon: Some had to be rewritten for production reasons. When they gave me the script, I said to Deke that he would be in trouble if we filmed some of it as written. There was no way I could have made it in the days we had. Then there was one thing where they were on horses. I believe they went off in the air or something ... it was fantasy, something to do with horses, if I remember correctly! I didn't have time. I never met the writers, but I am sure they were disappointed.

Ron: I've spoken with both of them, and Don Buday was the most vocal. One thing he said was that things could have been done to make the film look more evil than camp. He thought there should have been more day-for-night shooting; he felt there was way too much daytime in the film.

Gordon: These are technical things. To shoot day-for-night, you have to have some clouds; you can't just shoot into the blue. It's better — shooting at night takes twice as long, people trip over cables, they prepare for two hours before the light goes ... I hate night-for-night shooting. There's one shot, where Kiss are in a theater, where I should have shot day-for-night. It would have been so much better. I could have tented it off, and shot day-for-night. It would have been ten times better. I just didn't think about it, and it took all night to shoot that sequence *(this is presumably when Kiss fight the samurai)*.

Ron: Another big night shoot involved the "cybernetic creatures," climbing about the Colossus roller coaster.

Gordon: They used to put people on ropes, and pull them up and down. Looking at it now, the costumes are kind of comical; there's nothing that could have been less menacing. To his criticism *(Don Buday)*, this would be a great example where they put in the wrong costume, the wrong heads. You can't say anything on the set — you just have to do it.

Ron: As the project went on, how did you feel about it?

Gordon (laughing): I never really made a movie I really wanted to make! It's like writing pulp fiction, where you are being paid a penny a word; you have to do it and go on to the next one. If you turn down a film, you might be turning down two year's work. Let's face it; most television work is arduous for the writers. You get the script and think about how you can change things, and the producer is already working on the next one. As a director, you also need to get a script two months ahead of time, and spend four or five days with a writer.

Ron: Did you tell anyone at the time that you were working with one of the biggest rock groups in the world, who were also immensely popular with children?

Gordon: I've never been a rock and roll fan. I love classical and jazz music. But, the Kiss group, the essence of their message, was: "You're 13 or 14; you can do whatever you like. Sex is a part of your world." A shocking message, but I think it appealed to the audience that was there, but it was not indigenous to me. I was too old!

Ron: Not only were there the music and the message, but also the makeup and costumes.

Gordon: I think that whole theatrical effect of what they produced on stage for its time period was absolutely stunning. It probably still is. The concept of that was brilliant. But now, these characters are imported into a script, which is foreign to them, to what they themselves were doing. There were a number of elements interfering with each other. There are things, presently, in movie making, where people have eyes that can do damage. The film was very far ahead of its time.

Ron: Especially for a TV movie of the week.

Gordon: Yeah. And people weren't doing that kind of work, so there was something very "today" about it. Now, you have the Spider-Man movie. But, giving them these all superpowers through little gems was kind of hokey. It would have been much more intelligent — if you sat down with the writers — to come up with certain powers, and *why* they got the powers, and *how* they arrived, and *how* they disappear. Or, you don't give them any powers with little jewel objects; you make it much more invidious in the way you can eliminate these powers, or how they get them. It could have brought that to a higher level.

Ron: There was none of that.

Gordon: It was acceptable in television [the way it was done]. If I were invited to work with the writers on the script, I would have said, "Let's try and solve that, and make it better."

Ron: So you don't recall filming any kind of explanation.

Gordon: No. It was hokey just to have this silly, little box, which floats — ludicrous! It was probably acceptable then, but today *(laughs)* ... .

Ron: Do you recall Joe Barbera giving input?

Gordon: No, I just met him. Deke introduced him. He may have said something, but he would have conveyed it to Deke.

Ron: Besides wanting to replace Sam Cotton, one thing Deke mentioned was that Joe Barbera insisted on was Gene not sticking out his tongue so much, which of course was a big part of his shtick.

Gordon *(laughing)*: I thought that was great!

Ron: Deke said that Joe insisted on it appearing no more than four times in the entire movie!

Gordon: Yes.

Ron: He thought it to be repulsive.

Gordon: That's because he was of a different age. Kids love that. And he does have an extraordinary tongue. Barbera was so much older; he wouldn't even know what Kiss was about.

> "I think that whole theatrical effect of what they produced on stage for its time period was absolutely stunning."

Ron: How about some of other actors' performances? Carmine Caridi played an owner-operator type.

Gordon: These were really stock characters; they weren't very good. They were acceptable. The problem was, the people made a great mistake: if you are shooting a film, the best thing is to get the best actors. Then, you have no problems in your shooting. Instead, they try to save costs, and put in a favored actor. Though, the film was carried by Anthony Zerbe.

Ron: The best actor of the lot.

Gordon: Yes. You didn't have to say anything; he knew what he was doing.

Ron: Did he appear to enjoy the project?

Gordon: Shooting is so complicated technically, that he would just concentrate on giving something to his character, which he did very effectively, I thought.

Ron: Carmine felt he got the role because he underplayed it a little bit, as a contrast to Zerbe's character.

Gordon (*incredulously*): What *is* that role? It's a businessman. And he's trying to convince a guy, who is his partner, and is bitter. So, he's got to play a bit with the idea of convincing a guy about these people who are performing. If he had he been at higher level as an actor, he would instinctively known how to do this [fully] in his character.

Ron: Did you think this project would ever achieve any kind of cult status?

Gordon: No. All the films with Vincent Price have become cult things, and I get interviewed on them, and they are terrible pictures.

Ron: Did you think that back then about those projects?

Gordon: Yes, even then, I thought, *God, here's another one.* Vincent had such terrible lines to say. [In projects like this] the actor has to convince himself that it is the most important thing that they are doing. And as a director, you have to convince yourself that it is the most important picture you have ever made, and so on. Go in with that spirit, and get everybody excited. But, I had no idea. I was being interviewed by someone younger than you about a Vincent Price picture. I asked him what is the enthusiasm he has for cult films. He said he was brought up seeing them. I asked him if he had seen the classics, and he said no! Kids don't see *those* films!

Ron: So, the Kiss movie kind of ranks "down there" with the Vincent Price movies?

Gordon: Well, it's not really horror, is it? It's a camp script. You can't take it seriously. In a horror picture, you have to have *real* horror. People being buried alive, a divisive nature of a villain — that's really horror. But Kiss was for kids, for 14-year-olds, in my mind — that's where they were at.

Ron: Kiss has denigrated the movie in part by saying they had different expectations, and then were appalled after realizing it was campy.

Gordon: If you look at the dialogue, it's camp! But you can't just say, "Look, you're playing camp," and they couldn't analyze what they were playing, because they weren't actors. You don't have to tell Anthony Zerbe he's playing a camp style; he understands it. In fact, it's a bad word [camp] to say to an actor, because unless you're on a higher intellectual level in acting, like a fellow like Zerbe, you cannot do it. And, he had the seed idea of the character, which was correct. In directing, you should not really tell an actor how to do a line. The best thing was to give a suggestion; he comes with his bag of tricks.

> "There was something very 'today' about it."

Ron: It is interesting how there were no solo scenes for the Kiss guys; it would have been interesting to see them break off and do their own thing. They did that in their 1977 comic book.

Gordon: That was the script. The problems with the script, and there were many — and Kiss had recognized some of them, themselves — were that the writers did not have enough time to interview the members, to really get to know them. It would have been better, if the writers had that suggestion. It would have improved the script, to move them out, away from each other. Each actor would have had the chance to do his bit, other than doing a sampler.

Ron: How did you feel about the subplot of the mean trio of park attendees, the "crummy low riders"?

Gordon: If you look at it today, it's kind of comic book. Today, bad guys are *really* bad! They were sort of tame — it doesn't hold up.

Ron: The security guy characters were interesting in that they were sometimes made to be a bit bungling or goofy, and yet at other times, were written to be like full-on police officers.

Gordon: It was an age of innocence; there were not as many security people in parks then.

Ron: How much did you make for your services on the project?

Gordon: Maybe something between $40-60,000. Whatever the television rate was at the Director's Guild at the time, I would have gotten the minimum. They probably budgeted for that. What they are paying you for is to not have anything go wrong. If you get behind, and come on the set without-going straight into shooting, that $750,000 budget would go to one and a half million in a few days.

Ron: And with this project, you lost time at the beginning.

Gordon: Yes. You have to have a taximeter going.

Ron: So when you were hired, you went through the script to see what could actually be filmed?

Gordon: Yes, because people in television don't understand. Hanna-Barbera was an animation studio; they had no experienced people on this. At Universal, they had an expert on everything. An expert in projection ... Hanna-Barbera had none of that. That's why the horses didn't fly in the sky.

Ron: When exactly were the horses supposed to fly? When Kiss was on the carousel?

Gordon: I vaguely remember, yes, that something happened on the carousel, that was not in the original script. I do remember that there was a major sequence with horses.

> **"Their thing [Kiss] ... was to liberate you, into you feeling that you were very important."**

(How cool is this? This pre-dates Paul's mentioning on the Tom Snyder show in 1979 that he fancied himself "on a stallion, overlooking the Long Island Expressway." Perhaps he was partially thinking of this discarded scene/effect when he said that? Superobsessively, this Kiss-and-horses bit also comes before the lyric "stand the stallion and the mare" in the semi-heroic and overwrought "Odyssey" on the group's 1981 album, [Music from] The Elder. That's about it for Kiss and horses.)

Ron: Did you ever see the movie after it was finished?

Conversations with Phantoms

Gordon: This has been the first time I have seen it *(the author sent him a copy of the U.S. TV edit prior to the interview).* I didn't remember working on that film at all, after shooting it. You can re-edit it, and make it much better.

Ron: Do you mean doing a re-edit with just the footage that ended up in the final cut?

Gordon: Probably. You could do something more with it.

Ron: The overseas theatrical version has some extra footage, and some of it — particularly with the bad kids, serves well in further explaining what was done with them after being captured by Abner.

Gordon: They were subsidiary characters, and not that good, so that is why it probably was not used here [in the TV edit].

Ron: Were their abductions — when they were sucked up into tubes — just filmed in reverse, and they just jumped down and fell down on to mats or something?

Gordon: Yes.

Ron: All signs point to all the film footage probably having been destroyed by now.

Gordon: Some of the great classics are slowly disappearing — the Academy is trying to save a lot of fine films. Who is going to do that with this?

There was a bit of risk in the whole thing [for Kiss], but it was the sort of risk you would take. But the execution should have been on a higher level. It was limited, as you have four people that cannot act, basically. It's a great risk; I've worked for Hitchcock, for television, and maybe sometimes, you would have had a known singer play a lead role. The whole script is limited around that person, and it can easily destroy the thing. Here, you've got *four* guys, who have never done it. And you are asking them not to do sort of uncontrollable things, like not stick their tongue out. How can you make them play a sort of a role? Is it horror what they *(Kiss)* do? They're not playing horror, they're really just singing. Their thing — and again, this is what I got from their songs — was to liberate you, into you feeling that you were very important. The 14-year olds who were ignored — *you* are the powerhouse of the future generation.

Ron: That is a fairly accurate description of the Kiss spirit.

Gordon: The message that The Beatles had was at a much higher level. When you examine their songs, the intellectual level is stunning. It wasn't just for a young group [of people]; it was for a huge spectrum of ages. They were giants in their field. Kiss didn't have that level in their songwriting; it was showmanship. Utter showmanship.

PHANTOM FINDINGS
Which Kiss Member Has The Greatest Powers? The Eye Has It!

In *Kiss Meets The Phantom of The Park*, all of the Kiss members are shown to be highly skilled in physical combat, and have additional sets of supernatural powers mostly unique to each guy (flying is where things get nebulous). They appear to be in an advanced state of knowing what abilities they have, using them well and with confidence (that is, when they are not being drained by Abner and his ray gun).

The combination of the creativity of Kiss themselves (coming up with their characters in the first place), the scriptwriters' attention to detail, and the stuntmen's skills (and yes, a little cross-pollination from that first Marvel comic) made Kiss in *Kiss Meets* ... quite super heroic. Their collective skills are tantamount to a greatest hits collection of Marvel and DC characters! The Kiss members are not all equally equipped, however.

Peter/Catman is agile, and possesses skills such as judo and Karate style moves. He mostly uses rapid punches, but he also kicks, and has a takedown move that is seen twice. It's all pretty cool, but today, just about any soccer mom can do that stuff. He is surefooted, has fast reflexes, and can also leap impressively, which may be his only supernatural power. There is no Aquaman in Kiss, but poor Pete is close.

Gene/The Demon in terms of brute strength, Gene is the most powerful Kiss-er. Full-on punches are ineffective on him (very Superman), and he can also do some Karate-style defensive blocks. He rids himself of opponents by swatting and throwing them, but also uses generic kicks and punches. The Demon also employs evasive maneuvers like sudden upward flight (the only time he moves fast), and merely stepping out of the path of an oncoming attacker. He can also breathe fire (like Godzilla, though the big G's emissions are more toxic). It is sometimes seen as sort a warning — "I'm getting mad!" — and other times as a method of destruction.

Now is where the competition for who is the most powerful Kiss member heats up. **Space Ace** has the ability to teleport himself and the band through to different places — a very handy skill that can used to confuse foes, or even to just put some ... uh, *space* between them and himself and/or Kiss members. It also can save a lot of travel time. He can leap in a way that shows an almost otherworldly body control — he lands like an alien spacecraft presumably would at one point.

Ace is also acrobatic, and can somersault multiple times in a row — one time he is seen doing it after coming out of a cartwheel. He prefers kicks, and is seen doing some fancy fighting footwork. When he uses he hands, he delivers side chops more than punches (luckily his opponents are in the right position to make these work), and puts enemies in headlocks.

Speaking of his hands, he can also shoot beams and blast pulses of energy from them — he uses the former to make the Catman appear, and the latter to take out a couple of albino wolves and his evil doppelganger.

There is also reason to believe that Ace has advanced cognitive abilities and/or mental powers. Early on, after Paul eavesdrops on Calvin Richards and Snede, he says, "what do you compute, Space Ace?" Alas, these skills are only hinted at, as the reply is a Mr. Spock from *Star Trek*-like "insufficient data at the moment, Starchild."

Later, when trapped in Abner's lab jail, when Paul says, "we've got to get out of here," Ace replies, "leave it to me, Starchild — I'll bend these beams with my mind." From here, things writing wise get sticky; Gene says, "not yours," to which Paul adds, "ours." Here, rather late in the script, it is revealed that all Kiss members have telekinesis skills. Does it maybe only happen when they all lock in on a certain thought? It is not made clear, and from there, this happenstance goes from merely being convenient to not making much sense.

Kiss concentrates, but not on bending beams — they focus on retrieving their talisman, which have been conveniently left in the same room, unprotected, and together, in their cigar-style box. The box takes flight, passes through the energy beams, and into their hands. It's a great bit watching each Kiss guy coax the box in character, but it is perplexing. The group now has to be touching, or super-close to their talisman, to have their full powers? Earlier in the film, the things sat in a case at their headquarters while they went around the park, strong as could be.

Anyway, Space Ace sure has a lot of powers, but Paul has even more, making him the most powerful Kiss member! Check it out.

1. Paul can generate objects out of energy: Here's something evocative of the Green Lantern Corps: while the Starchild *flies* into Kiss' first performance scene, he decides to *walk* the rest of the way down to the stage (gotta get those steps in). Using his star power, he makes himself a ramp, complete with a chasing lights effect.

Related: While in the middle of the ramp, Starchild uses his eye again (multitasking alert!) to create an explosion of fire, within which, or behind which, the Demon appears! So, he can also make things and/or fellow Kiss heroes appear, or appear to make them appear, as they may be already there? It's not entirely clear. Note: Space Ace has basically the same ability, but with his hands.

Related to related: Speaking of explosions, Starchild's eye is also a laser gun, with settings somewhat on par with a *Star Trek* phaser. He can blow things up, but not entirely destroy them, but also can sort-of overload things to the point where they are destroyed and sometimes disappear. He shoots down a cybernetic monkey (after getting his aim under control), the evil robot version of himself (and it also vanishes), and even (with pinpoint accuracy, but only in the theatrical edit) a device placed on Sam's neck that Abner uses to control him.

2. Telescoping vision: Like Superman, Starchild can zoom in on things. A majority of the large amount of the zoomed-in area appears framed in a star shape, within which an orangey, sepia tone is applied to what whatever is being viewed (one hopes any evildoing he is monitoring is free of this hue; things like stealing old-time photos could theoretically be rendered invisible). Interestingly, in non-U.S. territories, his zoom imaging retains the original colors of whatever he is spying on.

3. Super hearing: While in telescoping vision mode, Starchild is showed to have enhanced hearing qualities, albeit in mono sound.

Related: I really wanted the following to be an example of X-ray vision, but upon watching it lots of times in both edits, it is Paul's super-hearing that is once again witnessed in the last scene. In Deveraux's lab, he is standing a few feet behind Sam slightly to the left, while Sam is actually half turned to the right, toward Melissa. As if hearing something no one else is (and they are all close together), he walks to Sam, and lifts back his shirt collar to reveal a device implanted at the base of his neck. In the U.S. TV version, he plucks it out with his hand, but in the theatrical edit, he once again uses an eye beam to blow it away.

4. Stupefying people: Starchild can seemingly mentally and physically stop folks in their tracks. Those placed under Paul's paralysis do not seem to experience pain, as at least one person (Snede) wears a blissful expression while under it. This actually may be kind of a riff on what The Joker has occasionally done to victims, most recently — to 1978 — in a 1975 Power Records *Batman* story (I know, that's a little obscure). It is hard to tell exactly how long Paul's grip on someone lasts — is it a spell with a certain duration, or a continually conscious hold on people? Next, how many people can it affect at once, and how does it exclude someone in a group he wants to read the mind of and interact with, like Melissa? After she starts talking to Paul, Snede appears to instantly snap out of it — was that due to Starchild releasing him? Meanwhile, the behavior of photographers around them indicates they too may be Starchild-struck, or maybe in a state of shock at what is going down before them. Or just bad actors in a rushed '70s TV movie.

5. Mind reading: When Starchild's right eyeball glows intensely, he can then aim and shoot one of his Atari Night Rider-style beams, and "see" what is on people's minds. He blows Melissa away with this skill, and while this power *is* pretty amazing, is not too hard of a feat with *this* chick; between her finance being abducted, Abner, Abner's lab, Kiss themselves, and their talisman, Melissa appears flummoxed more often than not in this movie.

There you have it: the Starchild is quite supernaturally gifted, and the most powerful in Kiss. Did the writers give him *too many* powers, with a minimal downside? Emphatically yes, especially when one considers the supernatural skills of the Catman, or lack thereof.

6. Physical combat: While his supernatural powers put him over the top — with them, he/Kiss can proact, and not just react, which is huge — Paul's physical fighting is also solid, *and* darn campy. When getting ready to engage in battle, he often adopts an inadvisable stance of putting his arms up in the air, leaving him wide open (think of what a gymnast does when presenting). In one scene, he strikes an alternate, equally farcical pose, putting both hands in the air to the side of his head, while making a glowering-meets-whimsical facial expression. It is a close-up made for screen captures — it almost like he is trying to make his attacker laugh.

It is commendable that Paul Stanley made the effort to come up with certain moves and poses to do when he is shown using his super powers. Here are a couple more: while he is making his way down his energy walkway, he does an overhead lassoing move (this is actually an on-stage move) and takes aim before making the explosion Gene appears in or from. When shooting down an albino wolf, he adopts a full-body aiming pose, that isn't bad at all — it makes total sense.

Carmine Caridi
"Calvin Richards"

Now for some old-school cool: talking with Carmine was much less an interview, than a conversation with a nostalgic Italian uncle. In stark contrast to the exasperated amusement park "runner" he played in *Kiss Meets The Phantom of The Park,* he was lighthearted, energetic, and entertaining. He ranks his *Kissperience* highly in his overall career, and his stream-of-consciousness style of remembrances certainly bore it out.

Ron: Wow, I'm talking to Calvin Richards, the owner of the park!

Calvin Richards, Uh ... Carmine Caridi: Was that my name? The odds of me getting that part were so far ... in other words, I played it differently — I auditioned differently. I did it softer, rather than loud. That's how I think I got it. I thought it was a nice piece. Anthony Zerbe was brilliant, and those kids were not bad for their first film. So, go ahead — shoot!

> "The spine of that movie to me was Gene Simmons."

Ron: To refresh your memory, filming was done in 1978 —

Carmine: — the year of my divorce!

Ron: So, you were having a fantastic year, already!

Carmine: How old are you?

Ron: I'm 30 years old —

Carmine: — I have ties older than you!

Ron: You had done a *Godfather* film; how could you suggest your chances were slim of getting a role in *KISS Meets The Phantom of The Park?*

Carmine: They were looking for certain qualities. I just took a shot, and played it reticent; I played it quietly.

Ron: I can see that in the final product. You also played it with a decidedly New York accent!

Carmine: That's also what I think they hired me for; I mean, I can speak without an accent. I went in and did it, and stayed with it. Why shouldn't someone with a New York accent own an amusement park?

Ron: I just got off the phone with Lisa Persky, who played one of the gang members, and she too spoke with a New York accent in the film. Then, there were the Kiss members themselves, most of whom displayed some New York accents. It almost seems there was a big "I love New York" vibe going on with this picture.

> "I didn't look down on them as actors."

Carmine: The spine of that movie to me was Gene Simmons. I loved that kid. We met in a supermarket right after that. He said to me, "You were great in the movie, I wasn't any good." I said, "Come over here, you big ... " and gave him a hug *(laughs)*. I told him to keep going, he could be one of the best villains. With Tom Selleck, he was a great one *(1984's Runaway)*.

He was dating Cher at the time — she was yet to pass him off to Diana Ross! We liked each other; we were both New Yorkers. I tried to teach him something, but hardly any of my scenes were with him.

Ron: Yes, they were limited. However, the pool scene is a total classic — you come over with your guards ... .

Carmine: I was first running over, slipped on my ass, and they all started laughing at me! I scraped my knee. I was like, "very funny, you f*cking freaks!" But it was a warm kind of union with these kids. I didn't look down on them as actors.

I thought to do what they do, they'd have to be good actors, you know? I told that to Jerry Vale, I told that to Al Martino, Frankie Valli. I said, "All you gotta do, Frankie, is transfer that emotion in what your singing — "just to good to be true" — to your acting. He was trying to find his way as an actor, and it was tough. So, I'd try to tell these guys who are great in another medium, that they could be good as actors. I just didn't go "What the f*ck am I doing with these bums here?" That was one of my favorite movies.

Ron: Really?

Carmine: Yeah. The one scene I remember the most was when I turn Anthony Zerbe around and he's dead.

Ron: Oh, the final scene.

Carmine: I turn him, and make that speech. It was very moving.

Ron: I actually have the script right here *(begins reciting)* ... .

Carmine: Anthony is an awfully good actor. He's so, so good.

Ron: In contrast of the overall nature of the movie, and the fact that Hanna-Barbera was behind it, it really seemed that the both of you actually underplayed your parts at times. The scene with him in the golf cart when you give him his pink slip is a good example: it is intense, without being over the top, and effective.

> **"I didn't get along with Paul Stanley."**

Carmine: Oh, yeah. I thought it was a very serious movie. I thought it said a lot about what could happen in a situation like that. Also, lots of people laughed at Kiss, but I didn't. I studied these kids; Paul Stanley, if you watched him, tried to emulate Gene Simmons, with women. Gene was going out with Cher, and, then he falls in love with Diana Ross! This kid Gene had depth. I told him, "Don't sell yourself short." They were in awe of Zerbe and myself. They looked at us as if we were *the* movie actors [on the set]. The kids didn't realize how much talent they had. I didn't get along with Paul Stanley. I didn't bother with him — not that he was a bad person, but you gotta be your own man. You can't emulate other people.

Ron: The group was really a study in contrasts; on one side, you had Gene Simmons, a straight-laced, driven person, and then Paul Stanley, who in some ways was almost like his kid brother at that point.

Carmine: Right. Exactly.

Ron: And then, on the opposite end of the spectrum you have —

Carmine: — Ace?

Ron: Yes. Ace Frehley and Peter Criss.

Carmine: Ace Frehley! I laughed so much at this kid! He was so loose — he didn't care. I don't think he cared about the film. A fun guy. The other guy *(Peter)*, I didn't pay attention to; he was kind of quiet.

Ron: He was reportedly somewhat withdrawn on set.

Carmine: If you compare them to The Beatles, he was like the

> **"Ace Frehley! I laughed so much at this kid!"**

George Harrison. Quiet, off to the side. Frehley was like Ringo. *(Takes off on a tangent)* Ringo was the least talented in the band; I wonder how they would have done with Pete Best.

Ron: Did you know that in the movie you never give the amusement park a name? You only call it "the park."

Carmine: If you say so!

Ron: You were telling me earlier about the pool scene.

Carmine: Well, I always had the two uniform cops with me. One of them was Brion James. They were perfect. I just played him *(Calvin Richards)* like a very rich amusement park owner; with power, and not very impressed with these kids. But in real life, I was very impressed with them.

Ron: I liked when you fired Abner Deveraux. You said: "You've been working too hard, Ab. You need to relax for a change. Travel. See the world —

Carmine: — get the fuck out of here!

Ron *(recovering from cracking up)***:** One funny thing is when you run into Abner, and initially express your dissatisfaction with him, you also tell him want to see him in your office, but you end up on a golf cart with him. I guess that was your office!

Carmine: Gordon Hessler got pissed at me a few times, because I was telling him how to direct the movie *(laughs)*. I said things like, "If I walk this way, and that guy is walking that way … ." I said I was just giving suggestions, and he ended up using my ideas, anyway! I think I could have directed that film!

It was very interesting; *(Gordon)* sees in me a guy who has played every gangster in the world. I had been acting about 16 years at that point. I was doing all kinds of stuff, like *Police Woman*. I was one of those guys who usually played a villain. But I tried to make this amusement park one different. I played him quietly. Because he *(Abner)* was nuts! Anthony Zerbe played him wonderfully.

> **"I think I could have directed that film!"**

Ron: You filmed on location at Magic Mountain, where the weather was fairly hot.

Carmine: Forget about it — we were dying!

Ron: You also shot in Culver City, where you spun Abner around in the last scene. Then there was that mansion with the pool.

Carmine: Yeah, it took a while to get out there.

Ron: Do you remember how much money you made?

Carmine: Very little. That's 1978 you're talking about. I was on *Phyllis* in 1976, and I only made $2,500 a week. Hey listen, you also do it for art's sake.

Ron: I pictured you as someone who would never want to talk about the Kiss movie.

Carmine: That would be unfair. I know they took a lot of ribbing for it.

Ron: Their then-manager Bill Aucoin was telling me that this movie was envisioned as a gateway project, part of a bigger plan. Kiss had the teen market at this point, and now, they were going to hook their little brothers and sisters.

Carmine: Oh, yeah. Kids loved them.

Ron: As they started to make the movie, it was perhaps due to inexperience that they didn't realize that they were actually making … a TV movie of the week. So, as filming went on, some members of the band felt the project was really hokey, and they were being made fools of, and so on.

Carmine: I could see that. I approach everything I do like it's the biggest thing on Earth, but I could understand. When I met that Gene Simmons, I fell in love with him.

Ron: Who did you actually audition for?

Carmine: Gordon Hessler.

Ron: Was it a formal screen test?

Carmine: No.

Ron: I dug your off-the moment attire in the movie. Did you wear your own clothes?

Carmine: I forget. Wait, was it a tan suit? I think it was my own.

Ron: One was, yes.

Carmine: I think one of them was mine, one was theirs. Did you talk to Anthony Zerbe yet?

Ron: He is holding out on me! Maybe he is still mad —

Carmine: — about what he did *(laughs)*!

PHANTOM FINDINGS
A Lost, Powerful Character

During the "Rip and Destroy" sequence, a freaked out Calvin Richards shouts: "Kill the power, Phil! Kill the power!" *Phil?* There is neither a "Phil" in the script, nor one ever seen on screen, or even mentioned, before this late point in the film. Still, Phil is mentioned, and as such, we have to believe that he exists in the Kiss movie world.

Here's what we know about him: he works with power. And, although he apparently could, should, and is ordered to by Calvin to "cut" it, but it is out of his ... power.

It is the not only time power control is compromised in the park, affecting the ability to cut it. In the early, seemingly interminable part of the movie (where is Kiss, darn it?), the crummy Lowriders sneak into a restricted area and override the controls for the spider ride, spinning patrons into an uproar. Snede and his men need to get on this lack of security around the park's power as soon as possible — people are probably running hot plates and ham radios off of it.

Don Lewis
Various Acting Parts
Interview conducted February 9, 2001

This interview was a lot of fun, and relatable, as Don and I share something of a similar background in doing live-gig entertainment. It's a style of performing that contains immediacy, demands flexibility, and if done well, fosters versatility — seriously. Additionally, when folks like us do everyday things like phone conversations, we tend to slip into entertaining mode — Don did so in our talk, making for not only a good listen, but also a great read about his work on Kiss Meets The Phantom of The Park.

By 1978, a 25-year-old Don had already done hundreds of shows as a street mime *(there was a time when this was huge, kids)*, stuff on cruise ships *(work that found him based in Hong Kong)*, and much more.

"I have no pride, I'll learn anything," he says at one point, only half-jokingly. He and his cronies ending up serving the Kiss production well — they played lots of memorable bit parts that greatly contributed to the flick's live-action comic book vibe. Gordon Hessler even remarked that he wishes he could have done more with them.

"And we weren't credited!" — Don

Don Lewis (about playing his punishment-inducing character in the Chamber of Thrills scenes): I just remember that I had this really *insignificant* whip. I knew how to do bullwhip stuff, so they said to me, "we're going to give you this whip." I said, "ahh, yeah, I am skilled — and this is *felt*!" Uh, okay. I also remember that Jan Stuart Schwartz (*a fellow performer*) was getting unhappy, because I was getting to whip *him*, and he could never hit *me*. Odd things, I remember about it.

Ron: How did you get involved in the movie?

Don: How this whole thing happened was, there was this guy, Richmond Shepard, who brought everyone together. He was like, (*adopts a classic, cigar-chopping, agent-guy type of voice*): "Do this [gig], and we will maybe have 10 percent [of the pay] for you, afterwards." There was also Peter Kwong, who was great in karate — he was a samurai. He did all of them, when they attacked.

Ron: Right — there were a few guys.

Don: But when the samurai attacked, it was Peter, and when they were just being robots, it was the other guys. I can't remember how much of this stuff was left in. It was really all Peter, though, and the thing I remember is that they [production staff] were all saying, "Can we actually have him kill himself in this movie?"

> "We saved them thousands of dollars."

Ron: You have a pretty good memory.

Don: I remember *some* of the things we did in it, but as far as what the film actually became ... we did *The Black Hole* — remember that horrible film?

Ron: Sure, it was a super-hyped Disney movie.

Don: I was all the robots that touched humans. And I don't remember the film at all, but I do remember a few of the stuntmen getting claustrophobia in the suits. Those are the things that I remember. In the Kiss movie, do you remember the crossed-eyed Washington?

Ron: Yes!

Don: Well, I can do that stunt (*crossing eyes*) far, far better than that. I can do it better, when I am *not afraid of being groped by the assistant director*! He was underneath that little table I was wedded into.

Ron: No way!

Don: Yes way! He was *extremely* friendly! He would kind of poke at you, kind of a pinch. And, Richmond is like, "well, if you can dance, *that's the way they think you are*. He's going to continue to be friendly, and you're not going to say anything." He didn't do anything *really* weird, but he was extremely friendly.

Those are the things that stick in your mind. Like, the fact that I stole a finger of Gene Simmons' glove — they cut it off so he could grab something. It was for my 15-year old brother at the time. For him, that was great. He was a heavy fan. That was probably the best thing I did, ever, as far as he was concerned. I also got him [Gene] to sign a card. I wasn't a big Kiss fan. I was there, basically, because it was a job.

"Anthony Zerbe was very nice."

Ron: How old were you doing the making of the movie?

Don: I would have been 25.

Ron: What point were you in your career?

Don: That's an odd thing, because I do — and am trained for — classical mime. In the '60s and early '70s, it was popular. The problem was, it was popular in certain areas. Then — and I can tell you the exact time — remember the movie, *Flashdance*?

Ron: Yeah, Jennifer Beals.

Don: The moment *Flashdance* hit, you could no longer do mime — in stories, anywhere.

Ron: Please clarify.

Don: Because first, the moonwalk, as you know it, was walking in place as a mime, and moving backwards. The first time I saw it was in places like Central Park. It was done so you could move backwards, but as not take your eyes off your hat. It was a cool thing to do, but it did nothing. Then, it became popular. But with *Flashdance*, all of a sudden all of the mime moves that used to be parts of stories became dance moves. It became impossible to do a mime story after that (*on the street*), where you didn't have nine kids come over and try to do the robot. I was making a hundred bucks a night doing mime stories; after that, I was basically being a white breakdancer (*Don actually appeared in Breakin' 2: Electric Boogaloo*).

Don: Could you hold on a second (*fumbles with phone*)? Oh, I think I lost the other call.

Ron: It must have been Jennifer Beals. By the way, Gene Simmons was supposedly offered a role in *Flashdance*.

Don: Was he? He could have helped killed mime — that would have made him happy!

Ron: Since you are a classically trained mime, during the making of the Kiss movie, why didn't anyone like Gordon Hessler simply have mimes fight Kiss? *(It is not that bad of an idea. Fighting mimes appeared in The Warriors in 1979!)*.

Don: Think of it this way: Terry Morse was the director, right?

Ron: He was the executive producer.

Don: I just know I was dating his daughter! We were there as non-union help, but I believe it was a union film. So, they would not have changed things based on us, directly.

Ron: Did you have a SAG (*Screen Actor's Guild*) card at the time?

Don: No, I was making more money doing live shows and such. And, I had done theater, and was a member of Equity (the "Actor's Equity Association," a theater actor's union). As far as SAG, no. So, we were on the thin line of being ... we were used for everything, but they did not want to pay us as union performers, because that would open up a whole can of worms. When they needed something, we did it. We saved them thousands of dollars.

> **"I had accidentally taken a picture of him with no makeup on."**

Ron: Do you recall how much you personally made for your *Kiss Meets ...* work?

Don: I made five hundred, to a thousand dollars. I remember that, because I took the money, and immediately bought into SAG. I had the right, because I was a two-year principal in Equity.

Ron: So, you got in off of your theater experience, and not your work on this film?

Don: Yes. As it was, we got no credit on the sucker, because we were supposed to be extras — but we were doing principal parts.

Ron: Let me make sure I have this right — the guy you were whipping was?

Don: Jan Stuart.

Ron: And, the gentleman who got you the job?

Don: Richmond Shepard.

Ron: And, he was a samurai guy?

Don: No, that was Peter Kwong. Jan Stuart Schwartz was Quasimodo. Richmond Shepard also actually did a little part. He was a guy in a hood, with a knife or an ax. Someone comes at him. Anthony Zerbe was very nice.

Ron: You actually had a significant amount of screen time with him.

Don: Yes, and he was totally delightful, the whole time. And, he was the only person to mention the fact that we were trained mimes. To everyone else, we were the extras. Except for Peter Kwong — when they saw him do his kicks, they said, "he's dangerous!"

Ron: I am thinking of his close-up.

Don: He has nice one, where he was lifting his sword, and he is doing a robot. I taught him that robot! We were all people that Richmond would call for jobs. There was Jan, Peter, and me. *(Okay, this Shepard guy was the guy that placed Don in the movie, along with the others just mentioned. Got it? It took the author forever to get it.)*

Ron: This job came straight from Richmond, then?

Don: Yes, but the fact that I knew other people was a factor — it was sort of a family thing.

Ron: I wanted to ask you about your audition.

Don: Ha! The audition was: Richmond said *(goes into cigar-chomping agent voice again)* "Okay, they told me to get some mimes. I told them that you guys are the best. Now, will you do it for this amount of money? No, it's not union. Okay, you're on." *That* was the audition.

Ron: Do you recall your first day on the set, and/or going in for a wardrobe fitting?

Don: I want to say we got sized at Culver City. I remember going over there and seeing the two biker guys there ("Chopper" and "Slime," portrayed by John Dennis Johnston and John Lisbon Wood, respectively). Lovely gentlemen, who told a lot of dirty jokes. They got sized at the same time we did. They took measurements, and did the costumes on set. I was measured for the monster thing, and I was measured for a clown.

Ron: You keep mentioning that you were a clown, but there is no clown in the final cut (those additional mentions were edited out of the above interview).

Don: Then they probably cut it out. I did like a mechanical clown as people walked by. Then, we did all these robot characters (probably the ape and astronaut exhibits). I vaguely remember being a security guard.

Ron: Maybe you were one in Gene's rage scene, where he breaks through the wall?

Don: Yeah, maybe that's it.

Ron: In the international version, there are a couple of more shots in that sequence. When one of the movie's main security officers calls for backup, two other guys show up.

Don: That is the sort of thing we would have been.

Ron: They don't show them that much.

Don: There were also a couple of other things where we were shot, but they didn't use. A lot of Peter Kwong's stuff didn't get seen. Like in the monster scene *(Chamber of Thrills)* where we attack them *(Kiss)*, and you see them kind of slowly going up, we were throwing punches at them. I am not sure a lot of that got used. I remember far more of the set-up of the "Washington shot." Somebody else was originally supposed to do that, and then I did my little eye trick. They really didn't care who did it — they just wanted a good Tory-looking guy!

Ron: Right. You *are* rather Tory.

Don: Exactly.

Ron: Do you recall how long you worked on the Kiss movie?

Don: I seem to remember one week. It could have been two weeks, but that would include getting hired, and having to wait to start the thing. Everyone got pissed [with the wait], because we had to give up jobs.

Ron: Did you meet Kiss during filming?

Don: Oh, yeah. And the one I spent the most time was Gene, because I had a number of scenes with him.

Ron: Yes, if you examine it closely, you seem to have your own little battle with him going on.

Don: I never thought of that, and I'm sure he didn't! In fact, I had what could have been a very valuable photo. I had accidentally taken a picture of him with no makeup on. I was really trying to get a shot of the director, but got also got a shot of him. I lost the photo, and my brother wanted to kill me. Gene talked the most. I talked to him about the fact that he was a teacher at one point, as at the time, I was teaching mime, at the American Academy of Dramatic Arts. He seemed like a perfectly nice person. I had worked with some rock and rollers, as a backup musician, and he was not what I was expecting. *Ace* was more what I was expecting. The drummer was nice. There was one guy who seemed out of it, pretty much all of the time. At one point, we were sure we could get high just using that guy's makeup!

Ron: The band was starting to come apart at that time, with members reacting to the pressure of their collective workload in various ways.

Don: I remember that they had recently finished a tour of Japan, and we watched the tape. Somebody put it through the monitors. *(This had to be a tape of the 1977 tour Kiss did there; let's not rekindle rumors about the 1978 run also having been filmed!)*

Ron: How about some Kiss gossip — did you see the guys arguing with each other on the set or anything?

Don: The only stuff we saw was that they were really happy that the stunt guys were getting punched. Paul was like, "let's make sure to get these guys Kiss t-shirts and stuff." They seemed to be separate. Energy wise, it was, "Demon and Starchild, and the group." They didn't always look really happy overall, I will say that. To the same point, nobody does in that situation, until you're in front of the camera.

Ron: About that clown character that you remember playing, there were also a bunch of planned scenes, with astronauts.

Don: Oh, yeah! Jan and Heyward were supposed to do floating astronauts in that. *(this is likely a reference to Deke Heyward).*

Ron: Wow. They ended up standing on a platform, just moving their arms around a bit.

Don: How exciting. Yes, I think it was Jan, and he was pissed, because he wanted to do an actual stunt.

Ron: Among your credits, there is something that is remotely connected to the Kiss movie. A while after it, you did an emcee gig at Magic Mountain for the Batman show — as the Joker.

Don: Oh, God yes! There is a certain route you take on the live show circuit. When the street mime died, I started working on the cruise ships more. After that, when you get back, a lot of the performers work at Opryland, or Universal, or Knott's Berry Farm.

Ron: I was wondering if you had called Magic Mountain, and leveraged your having worked on *Kiss Meets The Phantom of The Park.*

Don (laughing): No — absolutely not. I was working on body suits over there, with a stuntman, and he recommended me. I also did the pyro for the thing *(the Batman show).*

At this point, Don gets a call on his other line. It is none other than H.R. Pufnstuf himself, Van Snowden, calling from Hong Kong *(at the time, he was working with Van, as well as Sid and Marty Krofft, on a project).* We end our conversation — lest we incur the wrath of Witchiepoo — and I rue never figuring what exactly his clown character was supposed to have been, or done, in *Kiss Meets The Phantom of The Park.*

Mary Kay Morse
Girl on Pyramid

In your author's early-2000's hunt to find *Kiss Meets ...* alumni, Mary Kay Morse was one of the first people found. Mary *who?* The "Girl on Pyramid," that's who *(know your Kiss Meets ... credits)*. The daughter of the movie's producer Terry Morse, Mary Kay appeared *(in a cameo/extra capacity)* in at least two short scenes.

First, she is in the opening credits; while Kiss is performing their signature anthem "Rock and Roll All Nite" superimposed over Magic Mountain rides and attractions, a Godzilla-sized Gene Simmons rises from inside the Colossus rollercoaster *(the tracks are in a semi-circle around him)* and sings to her and another female Kiss Army member as they look up, and dance-walk by. It rules.

The next scene is where Mary Kay earned her credit name. In it, she is part of a group of park attendees who are apparently so "high-spirited," that they have decided to forgo everything Magic Mountain has to offer, and instead, are spontaneously making a human pyramid out of themselves. "Girl on Pyramid" is seen excitedly taking her place on top *(but she is not as excited as that one guy a row below her, whose mannerisms of excitedness make him seem like he is one of Abner's robotic creations)*. Her lofty position does not last for long *(but her name will remain)*, as true to *his* name, Chopper chops them all down with a left-foot sweep to the right arm of a guy on the lowest row *(He must have really known the structure's ultimate weak point, because his move is super effective. It also probably was not his first time doing such a diabolical act, but you know what? These pyramid people were in everybody's way, anyway.)*. After her fall, "G.O.P." shouts *(no, make that "verbally hurls")* "crummy Lowriders!" at him.

My talk with Mary Kay was as brief as her scenes — I was actually calling her to get contact information for her dad, and she was in a hurry. We made plans to circle back for a full-fledged *Kiss Meets ...* convo, but you know the deal with this project. Given her coolness on camera and the phone, our short exchange seemed worthy of inclusion.

Ron: I have the script in front of me — you're on page four!

Mary Kay: That's me!

Ron: So, when you were being the "Girl on Pyramid," were you with extras?

Mary Kay: Yes, those were all extras; it was controlled.

Ron: I just heard, as the "Catman," Peter Criss was supposed to be a master of kung fu, and apparently he was punching his stunt double (who was also playing his doppelgänger) full force!

Mary Kay: I can believe it! Stunt guys take beatings sometimes!

Ron: So, you pretty much hung out for this whole thing?

Mary Kay: Yeah, I did. Most of it, I was there. I remember being there one night. It was so windy, it sounded like something was falling from the [Kiss] stage. I also remember Ace riding his little minibike around the park — he was always taking off, leaving the set. They [Kiss] kept to themselves.

Ron: You have really made your mark in the makeup art world.

Mary Kay: I wanted to be a makeup artist since I was really young, and I think it was from being on sets with my dad. I thought it was cool, and was like, "Wow, you get paid for this?"

Ron: So, did you help Kiss with their makeup at all?

Mary Kay *(laughing):* No!

PHANTOM FINDINGS
Oddities and More

Melissa's Mouthpiece

It appears that Deborah Ryan is wearing something over her upper row of teeth throughout the movie. It seems akin to a mouth guard to prevent grinding (did they have those in the '70s?), but probably is some kind of primitive teeth enhancer.

Carmine's Suit Switch

In a movie where continuity was not exactly a strong *suit*, Calvin's blazer and shirt changes from the beginning of "Rip and Destroy" to the end of Kiss' on-stage fight against themselves. That whole sequence is supposed to be happening continuously, in real time, but nevertheless at the end of it he goes from wearing a navy jacket to a tan one, and he switches from a striped dress shirt to a non-striped number. The probable reason for this happening was that Carmine Caridi was at the Magic Mountain Kiss concert for filming, as well as the next day when more stuff was shot on and around the stage.

Calvin Richards Can Care Less

It's kind of neat that until presumably the end of the movie, when he sees them fight the phony Kiss, Calvin Richards is ignorant of Kiss' supernatural aspects. He just sees them as rock group with a big following that is going to bring a lot of money into the park, which is suffering from "terminal deficits." On a related note, it is established that both he and Abner are millionaires. Maybe the guys made their money elsewhere.

Office Location Confusion

When he has had enough with Abner and his trying out of the turbine engines, Calvin tells him he wants to see him in *his* office. The next time he sees him, at the ground level entrance to his lab, he says "you weren't in *your* office — I waited for you an hour." The two end up having their meeting in golf cart-type of vehicle, with Calvin at the wheel, in front of the Kiss stage, which must make Abner even crazier.

Sam's Bandage

In the final scene in Abner's lab, Sam has a bandage on his neck in the general area where Abner's electronic controlling device was before Paul pulled it out. One has wonder if there a small first aid scene filmed. Or, maybe the actor (Terry Lester) suffered a scratch or rash from wearing the prop? The editing in *Attack of The Phantoms* attempted to completely ban the bandage with a tight crop on Sam and Melissa when Sam recovers. If one looks *really* closely before that, after Melissa shouts "give him back to me!" at Abner and then makes her way to Sam, the bandage can be seen ever-so-slightly above his shirt collar.

Abner's Elevator

When Melissa is looking for Sam, she ventures into a "restricted area" that happens to contain the entrance to Abner's laboratory (the sign saying so over the door is very Batcave). A sensor detects her. Abner gets on a microphone and tells her she is in a "restricted area," but after learning what she is up to (looking for Sam), he decides to see her. He activates his "elevator mechanism," and tells her to step inside (You don't really want to know about how there is a different shot of this in each edit, with the back wall of the elevator interior in the TV version being both orange and red above ground, but all red below it, right? Oops.)

We next see her arrive in Abner's laboratory looking a little out of it, and deservedly so. Abner tells her, "you've just descended 150 feet in 2.8 seconds" Melissa tells him "someone could get 'the bends' coming down in a thing like that." Abner defensively and dismissively chuckles and responds: "not the way I designed it."

Let's do some quick math: $150 \div 2.8 = 53.5714286$

Melissa traveled over 50 feet per second, at almost 35 miles an hour! The UPS guy must *love* making deliveries to the lab (by the way, there is a UPS truck in the parking lot during the scene when Calvin "retires" Abner).

Our Phantom Fathers added a nice touch of sci-fi here, but Melissa's departure reveals an oddity: the "elevator mechanism" may only work with such speed when descending — as it takes her up, it is moving at a really slow pace!

Tal-eees-What?

In 1978, "talisman" and its plural form "talismans" were not commonly used words. They remarkably are still not today, even after being used in *Kiss Meets The Phantom of The Park*. Maybe the movie's varying incorrect pronunciations of them have abetted their obscurity?

For starters, both Gene and Abner say "talismen" for the plural form, but it is Melissa who takes the cake.

No less than two times — once for each time — she annunciates the second syllable with an "eees" sound.

The first time, where she should be saying "talismans" she says, "tal-EEES-men":

"They're un-REAL! I'd heard about your tal-EEES-men but I didn't think they really existed."

After doing some more of her patented overacting with her eyes, she can be heard over Abner's security pass microphone she can be heard making the "eees" sound again, this time even more pronounced:

"Too bad everybody doesn't have a tal-EEES-man."

It's almost like Deborah Ryan was going for a Jamaican accent — **"I'd heard about your tal-EEES-men, mon"**!

Side note: there is also line from Paul here where he reveals that everyone has a talisman, but they just haven't realized it. There is no point to this line existing for the story — it just kind of hangs there. But wow, the writing possibilities! Is everyone a superhero, waiting to be activated, upon discovering his or her talisman? If they find it, do they take on the appearance of a Kiss member?

Another Costume Head

You may recall the identification of two Hanna-Barbera characters' costume heads in Abner's lab in the James Hulsey interview. There is a third one that can be seen at

15:48 in *Attack of The Phantoms*. Look for it on the top of the bookshelf in the back of the scene — what is that?

A Lost *Power-*ful Character

During the "Rip and Destroy" sequence, a freaked out Calvin Richards shouts: "Kill the power, Phil! Kill the power!" *Phil?* This one was given its own *Phantom Findings!*

The Indecent Samurai

You can blame the costume — after fighting with Kiss the robotic warriors can be seen from behind, and you can see one of their behinds. It's at 1:03:25 in *Attack of The Phantoms*, and 1:08:03 in *Kiss Meets The Phantom of The Park*.

Abner Deveraux, Wisenheimer

The amusement park madman has some great lines throughout the movie, but two quick ones that tend to be overlooked occur in the scene when he is talking to the captured Kiss. When he tells them has changed their lyrics for the fake Kiss to sing, Paul asks, "in what way?" Abner shoots back, "*My* way." Before he departs, he tells our heroes that he has arranged for them to have front row seats to watch the phony Kiss, and rotates his work console. He then smugly says with a smile, "gentlemen, enjoy *yourselves*." Get it?

Kiss' "Kill" Count

The group's battle scene at the Colossus against the cybernetic monkeys/albino wolves is your author's favorite — it looks great, is fast-paced, and Kiss seems to be into it. Of course, they emerge victorious, but just how victorious?

Here's their "kill" count in *Kiss Meets The Phantom of The Park:*

Space Ace: 6

Peter/Catman: 4

Starchild: 4

Demon: 1

Total band robot take-outs: 15

Note: to qualify as a "kill," a special effect (video and audio) must be present.

Michael Bell
The Voice of The Catman
Interview conducted March 11, 2001

If you grew up any time during the last four decades and watched cartoons, Michael Bell is someone you have heard of, literally. Although his resume of on-camera acting work is significant *(and, choice — he did a couple of episodes of Cannon, and also appeared in David Cassidy: Man Undercover)*, it perhaps pales in contrast to his run in voice work, which pretty much includes a little of everything. A selected list includes franchises such as *The Superfriends (including "Gleek"!), The Smurfs, G.I Joe, The Transformers*, and even video games, such as the *Warcraft* series.

On top of all that, and of the highest importance for this book, he has also technically been a member of Kiss. He was the voice of The Catman, Peter Criss in the entirety of *Kiss Meets The Phantom of The Park (barring, of course, the scene where the group's song "Beth" is featured — that would have been strange if he overdubbed that)*. Although his voice is not naturally like Peter's, Michael perfectly matched his mouth movements, and delivered his lines in a fun and clear style, which actually elevated the character's overall acting. In fact, the combined efforts of Peter and Michael may have made the Catman the best acting Kiss character in the movie!

Ron: I noticed that *Kiss Meets ...* is not listed in your credits online.

Michael Bell: No, it's not. I don't know why. I didn't set those credits up, and actually, I have been credited with things I didn't do!

Ron: Honestly, what haven't you done?

Michael: I haven't done anything lately, except for *Rugrats*. I think I may be considered one of the old guys; I may not have the sensibilities of the kind of comedy that is done now. I do *Rugrats* because it is warm.

> " ... his acting was just a little bit off ... a little strange."

Ron: It is a huge franchise.

Michael: We just did *Rugrats in Paris*.

Ron: It has been a long run for that show.

Michael: I am hoping it runs as long as Scooby Doo.

Ron: Do you work with Mark Mothersbaugh? (*Mark is one of the brainchildren of Devo, who has also gone on to do lots of scoring, including Rugrats.*)

Michael: Actually, I met him for the first time doing he first movie, and then in Las Vegas, at the Paris Hotel, when were there or the premiere of the second one. He is dark guy — very dark. I would not let him babysit my kid.

Ron: I have heard that.

Michael: He was with Meat Loaf, I think.

Ron: Actually, he was with Devo. Besides voice work, you have also been on camera. I saw *Rollercoaster* listed in your credits.

Michael: That is kind of an underground movie, today. I played a feature role in it.

Ron: Like in *Three's Company*.

Michael: I did two of those.

Ron: How did you get into being a voice actor?

Michael: Well, the transformation was easy enough, and it is much more fun. I didn't find the roles I was given on camera to be satisfactory. In voice-over, I got to play characters that I would never play on camera.

Ron: On camera, you were doing smaller parts.

Michael: They were guest spots. I ended up playing some bigger roles, not juicy, but a lot of dialogue. I wasn't satisfied; I couldn't use dialects — I wanted to play dwarf drag queens! I really wanted to stretch, but I couldn't. I played what I looked like — a tall guy — so I played either the "bad guy," or "FBI agent." I was going with somebody at the time who was one of the top voice people in the business, and she said, "Why don't you do what I'm doing?" She thought I did it better than most people in the business. She dragged me in, and I got to work with Noel Blanc — Mel Blanc's son — and he hired me. I found my self working with Mel, Gary Owens ... .

Ron: Masters of the art.

Michael: And it was fun. I didn't have to worry what I looked like, like stars, who worried about how their hair was set, and how their teeth looked. I was really enjoying it.

Ron: You wouldn't happen to be referring to any cast members of *Three's Company*, would you?

Michael: Probably.

Ron: Suzanne Somers?

Michael: Yeah. Somers was difficult, to me. I found her ungiving. She was not there for the other actors, in my point of view. I found her somewhat distant, and at one point, we were working at something, and just before we were ready to roll, she said, "What's my line?" It wasn't the rule of thumb, but I unfortunately I ran into it enough times to say she was really dreary.

Ron: Would you say your voicing techniques were an outgrowth of observation?

Michael: Oh, yeah. All the stuff I did also came out of observing. I was always able to imitate people, observe, listen. I had an ear for it.

Ron: It seems like your voice work career was picking up steam around 1977. Of course, there was a little film called *Star Wars*.

Michael: When Leia is finally saved, a gray-haired man says something like, "Princess, thank God you are okay — we were worried about you." They had me dub him. I also dubbed somebody at the council. Lucas said he wanted me to dub this guy who's English — he says something, and Darth Vader looks at him, and he begins to choke up. I dubbed it, turned around to Lucas, and he said, "This guy is good." I was happy to dub it, but I thought the picture was awful! Lucas said to me, "Well, it's an action picture." I saw a work print, with nothing in the actor's hands, and Mark Hamill, who I now know quite well, was not particularly good, and I never thought Harrison Ford was good in those films. I just thought, *God, what a bad cast* — except for Alec Guinness, who was brilliant. *What is this film?* I am watching it in black and white, a work print, and Lucas says it's an action film. I said, "uh, okay."

But I told him the guy I dubbed was really good, and it would be silly to use my voice. He said there were too many English people in it, and I told him that he *did* film it in England! I did do it with an American accent, but he ended up keeping the guy's voice in. He used mine for the other character. So, years later, when it came out on videocassette, I was not able to collect!

> **" ... I didn't want to make it cartoony."**

Ron: This was pretty close to the time of your work on the Kiss movie. Do you recall how you were contacted?

Michael: It was just a job. I was called in to dub — they said it was somebody in Kiss, and I was familiar with the group. They played his voice for me, and he had a sibilant s.

Ron: A what?

Michael: A "sibilant s" — it just sounded odd on camera. It also just sounded a little lighter than they wanted to him to sound. They wanted him to have a little more testicularity or something, I guess! That was the impression I got.

Ron: How was it presented to you? Did they say that this guy doesn't know he is being overdubbed? Or that they just wanted to clean up certain things?

Michael: They just said that I was going to dub him.

Ron: They made it clear that you were going to dub all of his lines, in their entirety?

Michael: Yes. They played him for me, and I could see where they were going, because he was just light for the look with his own voice, and his acting was just a little bit off. It was *(thinks for a moment)* ... a little strange.

Ron: With your talent in the mix, the Catman character became much more memorable.

Michael: Thank you, I'm glad to hear that.

Ron: You can actually understand the lines, and the way you delivered them combined with the way Peter Criss acts and reacts, kind of gelled nicely.

Michael: Then it's a symbiotic relationship that he's not aware of! It happens sometimes. And, you have to understand from my viewpoint, that it was a job. You don't put too much credence into it, except expecting that someone is going to pick up the phone after something comes out and say they are going to hire you for future work.

Ron: Since you had a working relationship with them, I am assuming that Hanna-Barbera reached out to you, right?

Michael: I think it was them.

Ron: What did you get paid?

Michael: Oh, God - it must have been two Fig Newtons and a Chicklet! I can't imagine it was a lot.

Ron: Well, it was Kiss, it was Hanna-Barbera, and it was a movie of the week.

Michael: Yeah, but still ... I think it was scale.

Ron: How long did you work on the movie?

Michael: I think I did it in a day.

Ron: Walk me through the voicing process.

Michael: They had a reel on a screen to do ADR — I actually forget what means *(in the TV and move biz, it most commonly stands for "automated dialog replacement")*. You stand in front of a huge screen, and there's an engineer. He runs it once or twice — just the scenes, not the whole thing — and you have cans *(headphones)* on your ears. You have the script in front of you. You go line-by-line, word-by-word.

Ron: Until you get it right.

Michael: It's a combination of acting and syncing. A good sync is getting "the music" of a voice; I'll get the speech pattern.

Ron: This whole experience must have been a bit different from doing a cartoon.

Michael: Oh, yes. When doing a cartoon we just would do it first, before the cartoon was made. We did it like a radio show. You create, and then they do the work around you.

Ron: With something like *Superfriends*, you would be basically be doing it like a table read?

Michael: Yes, we used to sit around a table and go through the script first. I did two or three voices besides the main voices, you know, the "old farmer," or "crazy man who sees a spaceship." You would have to come up with those characters. Then, you have three characters in your bag, and you have to be ready to go. Then you do it, like a radio show. Today, like with *Rugrats*, we just do a small piece of it [at a time]. It's easy; when you have an animated show done, and you have to drop your voice in, that's a killer. You can't go any further than the parameters that are already there. It's the same with film. With Kiss, it was easy enough.

Ron: Do you recall who you worked with on the Kiss project?

Michael: I don't. When we work, we are in "mental cubicles" — we are not part of a group. We hardly meet each other.

Ron: Did you ever meet any of the Kiss guys?

Michael: No, as my work was all post production.

Ron: Did you do any other work on *Kiss Meets ...* besides the Catman?

Michael: That was it. I *may* have done possibly some subsidiary voices. I *might* have helped with the crowd while I was there, but that is just a throwaway. I was just there for Peter's voice.

Ron: What are your memories of the movie?

Michael: I remember rides, and people jumping around. I really wasn't sure what it was about, since I saw it in fragments.

Ron: About Peter's character, he was a "Catman," but in this production he was sort of turned into a *swashbuckling* cat; there were many pirate-like lines, like "aye, me bucko." Were you involved in any further developing any aspects of the character? How did you arrive at using the voice you used?

Michael: I tried three or four elements, and it's as close to him as possible. I didn't want to stretch too far, because I didn't want to make it cartoony.

Ron: So you did try a few different approaches?

Michael: Oh, yeah.

Ron: The story put forth by Kiss members Gene Simmons and Paul Stanley is that Peter's voice was replaced because he refused to show up for looping.

Michael: If that were the case, I'd be very surprised. I don't know if you ever heard him *(Peter)* speak, but he was light.

Ron: Peter's voice was perhaps too low-key?

Michael: He didn't have any energy. I'm a Brooklyn guy myself, and he didn't have any energy, and New York energy. He was *so* low energy.

Ron: He may have been tired from extracurricular activities. He physical acting was good, though —

Michael: — but acting is really dependent on the dialogue. The voice.

Ron: You have never seen *Kiss Meets The Phantom of The Park* in its entirety?

Michael: Never saw it!

PHANTOM FINDINGS
Peter's Pronunciation verses "Peter's Pronunciation"

At this point in *Kiss Meets ...* history everyone knows that voice actor Michael Bell overdubbed Peter Criss' voice. Being that by 1978 Mr. Bell's voice was familiar to the '70's kids that were watching this thing, it was probably a bit confusing — *that's* what Peter sounds like? It's also a bit comical, as its quality really stands out among Ace's squawks, Gene's harmonizer-effected lines, and Paul's alternating styles in delivering lines, such as his "regular" speaking voice, his really loud whispering ("let's go!"), and occasional yelling ("I don't believe it!").

Fans yearning to see and hear a version of the movie with Peter's actual voice are permanently out of luck. Luckily, an NBC promotional clip for the movie has survived and is on YouTube. This "bumper" (kind of a commercial and film trailer hybrid) contains a non-overdubbed Peter, delivering the following line: "apes is more like it."

Taken out of context, that line may seem like nothing special, and in context, it *still* is not — but it is all we have, making it an important artifact.

In his interview, Michael Bell asserted that the replacement of Peter's voice was due to his having a "sibilant s," which basically means he had a lisp (others have suggested that the kitty was also frequently tired, and may have not delivered his lines with the proper oomph). The promo spot contains two instances where we can listen for sibilance and make our overall own judgments on Peter's voice (and debate them on Facebook).

So how does the Catman sound? In this author's opinion, in this case, it seems his pronunciation of the letter s in *apes* and *is* was just fine. Moreover, he delivered the line in a way appropriate for the scene, at an acceptable volume level. In short, he nailed it.

What is interesting is that Peter and Michael Bell actually spoke their lines in a similar fashion; Catman dips slightly in tonality toward the end ("like it"), but in a natural way, while Bell keeps things on the same level throughout the line, making his version a tad more cartoony.

To draw your conclusions most effectively, I have created a video containing both versions of the line and posted it on YouTube — search for "Conversations With Phantoms: Comparing The Catman's Voice." Make *your* voice be heard in the comments!

Lisa Jane Persky
"Dirty Dee"
Interview conducted 2002

Lisa's Greenwich Village punk roots served well in bringing the nefarious "Dirty Dee" to life on TV screen *(talk about great casting!)*. She also interviews well, and in our talk we scoot around topics, amusing ourselves. Sometimes, it is like we are actually in the Kiss movie, with her of course being in character as 'Dee, and myself being perhaps some briefly interacting extra. In the great Kiss debate of who is cooler, Dirty Dee or Melissa *(okay, maybe that has really only happened in my mind)*, it's a no-brainer: it's Dirty Dee — and Lisa — all the way!

"I thought that Kiss was the most tragically unhip thing in the world."

Lisa Jane Persky: So, what do you wanna know? It seems like only yesterday. No, it seems like quite a while ago!

Ron: I'm this writer guy, see, and I'm a member of Kiss Army —

Lisa *(sarcastically)*: — oh, you are?

Ron: — and I always wanted to write something about Kiss, but wanted to be able to have fun with it. I have always loved *Kiss Meets the Phantom of The Park*, and with its inherent kitsch factor, it is a good fit for me and my pen.

Lisa: Right.

Ron: It also is a notable event in Kiss' history, and actually is just a cool '70's pop culture production.

Lisa: Interesting, and it is.

Ron: So, you have heard that on your end?

Lisa: One of my friends — who is becoming a lawyer — it's like his favorite movie! I mean, we think we do things that are meaningful, but this is the kind of stuff that is plain fun.

Ron: This movie is definitely something of a cult classic. For Kiss, this project was the straw, or one of them, that broke the camel's back.

Lisa: Have your spoken to Gordon Hessler?

Ron: Yes. But you, Lisa Jane "Dirty Dee" Persky, have the distinction of being the first on-screen person that I have interviewed!

Lisa: How about the other two guys that were —

Ron: — members of your gang?

Lisa: Yes — didn't we all have three names? I remember that. It was before the rash of three-named actors, and I was like, "Eww, should I get rid of my third name?" I was totally into the whole punk thing. My boyfriend was in Blondie *(Gary Valentine)*. So, I thought that Kiss was the most tragically unhip thing in the world. But I thought it was kind of a hoot. Since I grew up in New York, I remember early on that they played Kenny's Castaways. And he [Gene] was like, "We never played there." I was like, "Uh oh, I'm going to just not say anything." I do vaguely remember that there was a lot of tension. I thought that they didn't know what exactly was going to happen with this movie; was it a *movie* movie, or was it going to be a TV movie?

> "The Ramones were the *only* punks; everybody else was a pale imitation."

Ron: The legend is that KISS themselves were sold on the idea that the movie was going to be more of a *film*, but as filming went on, they realized it was not to be.

Lisa: Right.

Ron: They also weren't actors, and not used to getting up super early to report to the set. This came after a somewhat insane and non-stop four years of rock 'n' roll.

Lisa: When we shot at Magic Mountain, it was 104 degrees. I was all in that leather —

Ron: — ahh, that cool lightning bolt jacket!

Lisa: Yeah, and it had a cock ring on the shoulder, and I remember thinking, "Ooh, if I can get away with this ... " I had that jacket since I was 13. I wore it for years.

Ron: Now, when you filmed those outdoor scenes, you, Chopper, and Slime —

Lisa: Yes *(laughing)* ... .

Ron: — were the "Lowriders," vicious thugs, out for a bad time in the park.

Lisa: Indeed.

Ron: When I spoke to the scriptwriter guys, they told me that they actually based you on Chicanos, Latin gangs.

Lisa *(shocked)*: We were NEVER told that!

Ron: Maybe they kept it on the down "low."

Lisa: That was not even a rumor! That I would remember; I would be like, "Now, *that's* racially insensitive!" First of all, my take on it was that it was very much like a comic book, and we didn't really belong to anything, except the world of the movie. There was no backstory that we actually came from the ghetto or something.

> "It occurred to me that death is near!"

Ron: I was surprised to hear that, too. Was Chopper supposed to be your boyfriend?

Lisa: Uh ... I would have to remember!

Ron: Let me help jog your memory: filming happened in May of 1978. What were you doing prior to landing the Kiss movie?

Lisa: Let me think *(mumbles incoherently, as if thinking out loud)* ... .

Ron: How old were you?

Lisa: One question at a time! I had just moved to Los Angeles, so it *(the Kiss movie)* was probably one of the first things I had ever done. Before, in New York, I was writing for *New York Rocker*, and taking photographs for that.

Ron: Were you a fan of the Ramones?

Lisa: Yes — the Ramones were the *only* punks; everybody else was a pale imitation.

Ron: I knew it. In the movie, you had sort of a punk look, like you were in *Rock and Roll High School*, as opposed to *Kiss Meets the Phantom of The Park!*

Lisa: I was definitely a new waver, and those were my clothes. I did say, "Hey, I have an outfit." I didn't see what they had. Those black boots that go all the way up? They were mine. The worst part of it was how hot it was; it was just excruciatingly hot. They had people putting Sea Breeze on my neck, and trying to cool me off.

Ron: Was the park open when you were filming?

Lisa: Yeah, I think the park was open. Maybe somebody else will contradict that, but I believe it was. I think they might have closed off certain areas *(cue Abner: "this is a restricted area!")*. I don't remember there being any big crowds watching us.

Ron: You were in about five scenes all together. In the beginning you guys were hanging out —

Lisa: — Anthony Zerbe gives us some passes —

Ron: — which you use later to go into the Chamber of Thrills, where eventually, you can't find Chopper. You're like, "Chopperrrr … Chopperrrr … " You just can't find him. And then, Slime … .

Lisa: Wait — did I have an accent?

Ron: Yes — you have a very heavy accent in the movie, and I was going to ask you if that was your natural New York accent.

Lisa: No — that was acting! I don't have an accent. I guess I thought I was a New Yorker! I guess that I decided that since Kiss were New Yorkers, I was a New Yorker. I believe that was my motivation, to be like those guys! Ya know, *blend!*

Ron: It was like a tough chick voice. How did you get this gig?

Lisa: My agent found it for me. I do remember meeting Gordon Hessler. He was a charming man.

Ron: Wow. What lines you did you read at the audition? I am wondering if perhaps you read for the lead role, of "Melissa."

Lisa: No, I did not. I wonder if I still have that script.

Ron: Do you still have your jacket?

Lisa: I don't. It just smoldered away. I wore it to death! I got it from a thrift store in '72, 1971, maybe.

Ron: Did you meet KISS on the set?

Lisa: Yeah.

Ron: With makeup, or without?

> *"This kind of thing was supposed to fun, and I remember thinking, wow, they're not having fun."*

Lisa: Well, I met Gene without. I met him one of the days I went for a fitting at that studio *(Culver City)*. That's where I got closed up in the iron maiden. That's where I saw him for the first time. I remember thinking, "God, it's so cool to see him." I always feel camaraderie with my fellow New Yorkers, but I don't think he felt that with me.

Ron: Really?

Lisa: Well, judging by his response to my mentioning Kenny's Castaways. I didn't think there was anything wrong with it, but he thought it was really terrible!

Ron: I have to say, in the Chamber of Thrills scene, do look pretty scared. It was a convincing performance. When you are looking around for Chopper, you have *had it*. You want out of there.

Lisa: It occurred to me that death is near!

Ron: Your scene, right there, really set an eerie tone for the movie.

Lisa: Good!

Ron: After you get captured in the iron maiden, they show you traveling through a pneumatic chute of some kind.

Lisa: Yeah! I am just recalling that. I had totally forgotten about it.

Ron: And there's a scream … .

Lisa: Ya know, I love to scream — I get to scream so often! I want to make a reel of all my screams, because I got to scream in so many movies. I scream in *Cotton Club*, *The Sure Thing*, and *The X Files*. Actually, there is some kind of similarity in those two *(Kiss Meets ... and her appearance on The X Files)* performances. But about the screams, In *The X Files* episode, the devil comes and takes my baby; [I am in] sheer terror. That was a "sheer terror scream." The others are "eeriness and horror" screams.

Ron: So, you worked on this movie for about a week in total?

Lisa: Maybe four or five days. Remember the laboratory? I was a pioneer woman. I remember it vaguely. How did he *(Abner)* get us? Did he hypnotize us? How did he get us in those costumes?

> **"I was actually given that part again ... I do have a similar part in an episode of The Incredible Hulk."**

Ron: You guys were sucked up into the tubes in The Chamber of Thrills. Then, three scenes later, he is working on a Gene robot. You get shown, standing there, dressed up.

Lisa: We're like frozen or something.

Ron: Judging by the script, you are now a cybernetic creature; he *(Abner)* has now linked you to his electronic controlling devices *(Lisa moans in an "uh-oh" fashion)*.

Lisa: Gary and I were comic book freaks; I liked DC and he liked Marvel, so we were into it — that part of it was very fun.

Ron: There is an additional scene in the international cut —

Lisa: — there are two cuts?

Ron: Yeah!

Lisa: No way!

Ron: In it, there is one extra scene where Chopper and Slime are shown — you are nowhere to be found — in their Revolutionary clothing, and go and gas a couple of security guards. I don't know why you weren't there.

Lisa: I was a real badass, wasn't I? I mean, wasn't I kind of the ringleader of the badasses?

Ron: I would give you that title, yes.

> **"I was a real badass, wasn't I?"**

Lisa: Okay, so what I am thinking is that Abner eliminated me first, because I was the actual ringleader threat.

Ron: So, the "Phantom" himself, not wanting any additional grief, simply took you out, off camera.

Lisa: This is in my own memory, of course.

Ron: Yes — I wouldn't want Chopper to come after you. Now, I picked up a lot of tension between Chopper, Slime, and Dirty Dee, though. You were in the middle of this triangle.

Lisa: Yeah, I actually thought and think that was interesting and unusual — don't you?

Ron: Yes.

Lisa: I was actually given that part again. I never thought of myself as stereotyped — there are these random things, like screaming — but I do have a similar part in an episode of *The Incredible Hulk*.

Ron: In 1979.

Lisa: I was there with another three-name guy. We terrorize a town stricken with E. coli, and of course, we eat food that has been lying around for some picnic, and we all die.

Ron: Hey, Hulk is a Marvel property!

Lisa: I liked them all, but I was a DC freak.

Ron: So ... I was saying that you were the leader of the gang, and at one point, you intimate to Chopper that he needs to remember who he "come" with, as he is preoccupied by a mechanical gorilla. Not only that, but Slime taunts you about it.

Lisa: Yeah, that's right. I get jealous, right?

Ron: Yes, and in the script — a copy of which is right here — it says you feign jealously, actually.

Lisa: Uh huh.

Ron: Yes — it is on page —

Lisa: — it says I f*eign* jealousy. It is not *real* jealousy; I think I may have played it like it was ... *actual*.

Ron: Well, maybe it was a poor take?

Lisa: Ya know, acting is supposed to be living truthfully, under imaginary circumstances.

> "I do sort of remember that Chopper was an important deal to me."

Ron *(in learning mode)*: Oh.

Lisa: Of course in this one, it was living dangerously under imaginary circumstances *(cracks herself up)* — that's what it is supposed to be!

Ron: In the beginning, you and your vicious partners kick down a pyramid of people —

Lisa: Uh huh —

Ron: — and you taunt them by saying, "and the walls come tumblin' down."

Lisa: I do remember this dialogue. I do sort of remember that Chopper was an important deal to me.

Ron: Here's what I get: Chopper was your lover of sorts; you were the king and queen of the Lowriders. And then there was Slime, the lovable sidekick, who perhaps was your brother.

Lisa: First of all, with this Lowriders thing, we really didn't belong to anything except the world of the movie. It was very much like a comic book. There was no backstory that we *actually came from the ghetto*. You know what I mean?

Ron: Right.

Lisa: You just get to spontaneously be, in a situation. You play this character, and before and after that, there is nothing. They *(the gang)* are just some badass backstory, weaving through [the plot].

Ron: In this movie, there are garbage cans everywhere. I am trying to figure out if is a metaphor for something; I just don't understand it.

Lisa: Wasn't I thrown into a garbage can?

Ron: Well, somebody gets thrown into one, at one juncture.

Lisa: That's what I thought.

Ron: Mr. Simmons — or rather, the evil robot Gene Simmons — bursts through a wall, and opens a can of whoop ass (2020 me is cringing at my using of that term) on a couple of guards. One falls into a suspiciously present garbage can. Those things are *everywhere* in this movie!

Lisa *(after totally cracking up):* You've *got* to talk to Gordon Hessler; you've just got to! I wonder if he's still alive.

Ron: That's what I am wondering; I wouldn't want him to talk to me from beyond the pale or something.

Lisa: You gotta call BASTA or something.

Ron: That's what I have to do ... what's it called, "bastard"?

Lisa: BASTA! That's what you gotta do.

Ron: About Gordon, apparently the writers were a little upset with him, and he was a little upset with Kiss ... there were a lot of diverse talents there, trying to squeeze out a TV movie. He had done *The Golden Voyage of Sinbad*.

Lisa: I was really excited about that. Gordon was a good guy, and was trying to make the movie as good as possible, in the short time we had.

Ron: Do you recall seeing any hissy fits on the set?

Lisa: I don't remember anything specific, but do remember there was a lot of tension and not a lot of happiness, which is not that unusual on a TV movie set. I remember feeling, I remember clearly, a sort of unprofessional feeling. This kind of thing was supposed to fun, and I remember thinking, *wow, they're not having fun.* On the other hand, these guys [Kiss] were not actors. Plenty of people that I met in the rock and roll world were like that. This is a different kind of hard work. Was I right?

Ron: Yes. Peter Criss and Ace Frehley were particularly not into it. Hey, did your boyfriend ever come to the set with you?

Lisa: I don't think he did. He was much more anti-Kiss, but he thought it was really cool that I was doing the movie, because of Gordon. We really thought, in our hip, CBGB world, Kiss was kind of a joke. But I was totally willing to take them seriously, and I was excited to do it.

Ron: How was it working with the Chopper and Slime guys?

Lisa: I liked it, and we really did hang out as a trio. I stayed in touch with Dennis for a while after that — he was a writer.

Ron: There is scene I just recalled, where you and the guys have messed with electronics and a ride is spinning out of control.

Lisa: Right. We are really bad people; we're *really bad*. We love being bad, too; no conscience. We are really lucky that we ended up the way we did *(as robot-types, under Abner's control)*, or we all would have spent years in prison.

Ron: Totally ruthless. It's really because of you three that Abner went on the loose, trying to destroy the park, and Kiss had to intervene.

Lisa: Oh, such power. An early example of Women's Liberation.

Ron: Did you ever include your scenes from this movie on your highlight reel?

Lisa: No!

Ron: You are still a full-time actress, right?

Lisa: Pretty much, but I am trying to go back to writing. I am working on a book about growing up in Greenwich Village. I don't know if I am gonna publish it, yet. Hey, do you have any kids?

Ron: Yes, I have a son who is nine months old. He hasn't seen *Kiss Meets The Phantom of The Park* yet.

PHANTOM FINDINGS
Most of This Movie is Garbage ... Cans

There is a reason this section is where it is, in this book — it may trigger some readers to finally believe the author has "gone Abner" (as some of us *Kiss Meet The Phantom of The Park* fans say). Conversely, and preferably, you may think I have made an amazing discovery. There is a fine line between genius and insanity, right? Left? Dead center.

By the late '70s, amusement parks were long filled with stands selling snacks and soda (such as the Coke that Melissa pounds at the snack bar while stressing out over Sam's no-show — more non-intentional product placement). People consuming all that stuff means more garbage, and by 1978, leaving any around was finally and thankfully on its way to going permanently out of style. As crazy as it seems, it was once a thing to just leave refuse just anywhere.

Multiple viewings of *Kiss Meets ...* have revealed a rather surprising, but irrefutable fact: there are garbage cans all over the place. They are in places that make sense, and then in spots that boggle the mind. The more you look, the more you see them. In fact, being on the lookout for them is like a whole new way of watching the movie.

Don't *throw away* my assertions, read on, and then see for yourself – "just do it, man!" The times follow the television edit.

#1 (3:19): Our first garbage can is on the right hand side of the screen during a camera pan.

#2 (3:20): At the end of that (rather sloppy) pan, a time traveler from the 1950s can be seen. He bends down to reveal this second can.

At 3:30, dig that quick glimpse of a blow up image of Kiss' *Rock and Roll Over* album cover — it probably is the exact one used for the spinning *RARO* in the opening credits.

#3 (3:47): As the Phantom Fathers subject us to another ramshackle pan shot ("just use all the pans for establishing fill shots!"), which follows a (poorly) running man and child, a can is viewable, and it apparently has limited access.

#4 (3:48): We are still in this pan, as the man hobbles and the kid runs past another can, which is out in the open. It's a safe bet this garbage can sees a lot of action.

#5 (3:49): Amid the gaggle of girls walking toward the camera, there is can visible between a lady traveling to the right on screen, and the first girl from the left in the aforementioned group, walking in the direction of the camera.

#6 (3:53): As Calvin walks with a majority of the parks' entire security force, trying to calm down that ol' fuddy-duddy Snede, who is definitely NOT a member of the Kiss Army, we get a side shot of a can, in the background, to the right.

#7 (3:54): Hey, there's another can, in the open, at the park's ticket booths.

#8 (4:03): This one is inside the park, seen from overhead — you have to really look for it. Bonus points if you find it!

#9 (5:20): After being blocked just outside the exit of The Revolution by the ginormous Canyon marching band, Sam and Melissa are standing near someone in a yellow, now vintage, and rad, Hawaii t-shirt — a can is peeking out from behind him. This same can is easier to see at 5:37.

#10 (5:56): While Chopper is being a menace (in his pink t-shirt), a can be seen sitting next to a snack stand.

That's ten garbage cans in barely six minutes — but who's counting? Oh, this writer is.

#11 (6:03): You can see a can between Calvin and Dirty Dee.

#12 (6:05): A garbage can is sitting all by itself. It is included in the zoom shot that goes from 6:08-6:10 to reveal Abner coming out from behind that "Kiss cut-up."

#13 (6:13): There is a garbage can inside the ride area (upper left-hand part of the screen).

#14 (6:45): The tippy-top of a can is sitting next a train cart that runs on popcorn. You can see more of it at 6:55.

This is also a scene when Calvin is wearing his best suit; a safari tan jacket with flared bottoms, white shoes, and a cool belt. Carmine Caridi mentioned that one of the outfits he wore was his — I bet this was it.

#15 (7:12): Look near Calvin's left arm to see the side of one.

#16 (8:55): After a short break, the cans come back! As Shaun Cassidy Guy (an extra who was used in some key extra moments) and his pals ogle Melissa, there is a garbage can viewable over his left shoulder.

#17 (9:16): After a nice shot of the Magic Mountain monorail pans to a Kiss merchandise stand, a can sits among the shopping Kiss fans. It is visible again at 9:21. Don't miss another appearance by Sean Cassidy Guy at 9:26 – he is in a different shirt that looks to be too big. He also checks out Melissa here as she walks off.

#18 (9:38): A can is sitting by a tree, near the Spaceland animatronic astronaut exhibit. A bickering Abner and Calvin walk between it and the space thing. With some people also there, it's a bit of a tight fit, and Anthony Zerbe comes close to walking into it! It is seen again at 9:55, as Abner looks at the flying Kiss banner with disdain.

#19 (10:01): After Abner and Calvin walk past a tree that does not appear to be indigenous to California (it almost seems to be like a Christmas tree), a can is waiting for them on the other side. Note: after being in the background most of the time thus far, the cans are being seen more toward the forefront of scenes. At one point, the shot almost consists solely of the two actors and the can!

#20 (12:41): As Melissa listens to basically an uncaring Snede regarding the disappearance of Sam (he really stinks here), a garbage can is featured (yes, it is becoming okay to call these things "featured") in the distance, to the left of and a little up from Melissa's shoulder. This can gets more screen time before and after Brion James' memorable "wayyyyy underground" line.

#21 (13:10): If you can see this sliver of one, to the right of Melissa, you are automatically promoted to Kiss Army sergeant staus.

#22 (13:36): This scene is incredible from a garbage can perspective, and the most blatant example of using them as both set decoration and props. Dirty Dee, Chopper, and Slime emerge from a control room to a small, off-limits area. There are *two* garbage cans in this space (one is crooked), within about six feet of each other, with the last one situated *at a dead end*. This area has the building one side, and pipe fencing and trees opposite it and in the distance. As Abner shows up from the open end and only access point of this area, Dirty Dee leads the gang's escape opposite of him (yes, into the dead end area). She is reaching for the first can, eventually places her left hand on it, as Chopper and Slime catch up to her. They all head to the dead end near can #2. On the way, Dirty Dee also checks the trees, as if looking for a way out through them. Was that Lisa Persky doing a bit of improv? These cans are briefly seen again as Calvin Richards hits the scene, asking Abner why people are being tortured on the spider ride.

Two side notes:

At 13:44, as Melissa arrives to check out the spider ride chaos, she slightly trips!

The overdubs of distressed riders are funny — "This has gone far enough!" is a good one.

#23 (39:44): When the biplane ride suddenly comes to life, jarring the security guys, a can stands behind them.

#24, 25, and 26 (40:07): At the very beginning of Fake Gene's rage scene (when he breaks through the wall), before he appears two cans of the now common kind are present, as is one of another style. As you now know, this scene was not filmed at Magic Mountain. As such, were those "regular" cans from the movie brought along for placement in this scene? It sure seems like it. Ahh, more evidence that these things were an integral part of set dressing.

At 41:30 Evil Gene forearms one of the guards, who then crashes into one of the familiar cans. That is two times one of the actors interacted with a can (the other time of course was Dirty Dee's reaching out and touching one). That technically makes them props!

Phantom Findings

#27 (59:59): At just about an hour into the movie, Abner watches Kiss on one of his teeny monitors as they make their way into the park by flying and leaping over a fence. They land just behind and to the right of a *large, industrial garbage can.* In reality, this scene was set up on the Colossus roller coaster's construction site. This can is featured in the monitor shot as much as Kiss! Was all this can stuff an inside joke of some kind?

At this point viewers get a break from the constant cans as the movie shifts to Abner's laboratory, which has not *one* ("Sam, take out that rubbish — *that* is not needed") and then to the Chamber of Thrills, etc.

#28 (1:18:40): This is where the cans come back, and lest anyone think your author's concept of garbage cans as set design is a *waste* of time, there is not one, but two, on *the side of the Kiss stage.* The first one seen is positioned at an angle —

#29 (1:18:42): — facing this one! They are only about three feet apart! Both cans are in the same frame at 1:18:47. How bizarre is the placement of these two trash cans?

Ironically, at 1:21:23 there appears to be some trash near the bottom of the stage stairs that could have easily gone into one of these nearby receptacles.

That is it in the TV movie for garbage cans, but one does appear in the closing credits (when your author saw it, he did an Abner-style "of COURSE"!). Look over Calvin's shoulder at 1:33:53.

This author apologizes for not asking art director James Hulsey about the proliferation of garbage cans. And for this Phantom Findings.

ABOUT THE AUTHOR

Ron Albanese first heard Kiss unknowingly and indirectly in 1976, when a fellow first grader sang "I Want You" to him. He would hear them directly for the first time in the summer of 1977, when his mother included the band's *Rock and Roll Over* album in one of those "choose 10 8-tracks for a penny" deals. He would request she play it whenever they were driving around in her Cadillac.

Like so many Kiss fans, his eyes were glued to the TV at 8 p.m. on October 28, 1978, to watch their TV movie *Kiss Meets The Phantom of The Park*. Turning up the 19-inch Magnavox console as loud as it would go, Ron was mesmerized. At its conclusion, he spontaneously made a giant Kiss logo with his hands in his family's recreation room shag carpet, and went to bed a now-permanent member of the Kiss Army.

Years later, after becoming a professional writer, and wanting to create a book related to "the hottest band in the world," *Kiss Meets ...* immediately came to mind. Ron did research, conducted interviews, and then took an extended break as other things in his life started happening, such as starting a family and a children's entertainment business. Years later, he came across the interview tapes and decided to finally put something together — the result is in your hands!

Contact:
KissPhantomBook@gmail.com

Facebook:
Conversations With Phantoms: Interviews About Kiss Meets The Phantom of The Park